THE GOVERNMENT CONTRACTOR'S

RESOURCE GUIDE

By

Daisy Gallagher

Published by

Access International

Fourth Edition 2009 ~ 2012

The Government Contractor's Resource Guide

© 2012 ~ 2020

Daisy Gallagher

ISBN-13 978-0-9789647-1-9

Library of Congress Catalog Card Number 2006907430

Disclaimer:

While every precaution has been taken in compiling this book, it is intended as a guide for marketing to the Federal Government and does not guarantee awards of Government contracts. Gallagher & Gallagher makes no warranty, expressed or implied, concerning the content, information, products or services detailed herein. Gallagher & Gallagher, Inc. will not be held liable for any action taken or not taken on advice rendered or accepted on the basis of the information contained in this book.

Note:

All information contained in this Government Contractor's Resource Guide is current as of December , 2010. Gallagher & Gallagher, Inc. is not responsible for any policy, procedural or informational changes made after this date

To All My Colleagues in Small Business:

Every twenty seconds of every working day, the United States Government issues a contract. The United States Government allocates $300 billion dollars for contracting. The small business goal is 23% of that amount. Do the math; that makes the United States Government the largest marketplace in the world and a great opportunity for you to grow your small business.

Those of us interested in contracting with the government and running small businesses need to absorb as much as possible in the short time available.

The information on government contracting is plentiful, but sifting through extraneous information to find exactly what you need is an arduous task. To ease the information-gathering process, we have assembled as much pertinent information as possible to help your small business obtain resources and avoid some of the pitfalls, time, money and frustration commonly experienced in government contracting.

We priced this book so all small businesses can afford it. We are not in the practice of consulting to small businesses on government contracting; we are a strategic marketing, branding and public outreach firm. We want small businesses to know that they can afford to get into government contracting because the government has FREE workshops, conferences, seminars and training available to them.

If you want to work with the government, you must adhere to best practices and provide the best value. You must be aware of your present limitations in contracting, specifically what you can and cannot do. For example, if your company has been in business for one year and your largest private sector client's budget for your business is five thousand dollars, you will become frustrated if you try to go after a million dollar contract.

Keep excellent financial records

After you have received certification, you must understand that you work for the government and therefore, you work for the public. So, it is only a matter of time before you are audited. You will be audited once or several times a year. GSA comes on-site to review its contractor's books. Therefore, you should always maintain excellent credit and financial records. Private industry knows that, as an approved government contractor, you must keep good records, so this in itself helps grow confidence when marketing to the private-industry clients.

Market your company

Now that you are certified, you must be proactive in pursuing contracts. The certification process is the exhausting first step into the maze of bids, contracting, statements of work (SOWS), requests for quote (RFQ), requests for proposal, (RFP), and potential clients. Even proper completion of every single form does not guarantee contract awards. You MUST invest in marketing your company to the government. This means a plan, including development of print materials, direct mail, making follow-up calls, attending trade shows, networking, relationship building, and searching for procurement opportunities.

Be persistent

Do not become frustrated. If you are good at what you do and invest in marketing your company, opportunities will come. You cannot become discouraged if you invest countless hours on a proposal and are not awarded the contract. This is the investment you are making. You must also know your financial limitations. Remember, you are competing with firms that might invest many thousands of dollars and man hours going after the multi-million dollar contracts without a guarantee. My advice is to prove yourself in producing quality work with smaller contracts and, sooner rather than later, word will get around. As large as the government is, it is small enough for word-of-mouth to be effective. Remember, procurement professionals all go to the same conferences, the same expos, and the same training. If a contractor is unethical in pricing by low-balling and then upping through other direct costs (ODC) after the contract is won, or does not hold up their end, it will prove in termination - and worse - word will get around. So, know that those who continue to grow customers in government are similar to firms that grow customers in private industry. You will not stay in business if you don't put your customer first.

Know your resources

PTAC are a phenomenal resource. They will work with you on developing proposals and are an excellent resource for answering technical questions. You should exhaustively question the assistance available from any source you contact.

For example, we had worked with our regional economic development council a number of times, but it was only after we were referred to our local PTAC that we learned they were one and the same. We could have received additional assistance several months earlier!

The SBA and Senior Corps of Retired Executives (SCORE) are two more great resources. SCORE was the first agency I went to before I opened my firm. These are retired executives with years of experience behind them, willing and able to help you in whatever direction you need to go, without charge. The Small Business Development Center (SBDC), housed in local colleges or universities, is another great tool.

As a woman business owner I have found helpful resources such as the SBA Women Business Center (http://www.sba.gov/about-offices-content/1/2895), which offers a myriad of assistance. This Web site offers numerous links to business centers, networking, and research specifically geared toward women-owned businesses.

Also, know how to use the GSA. Be active within the GSA and develop a relationship with your GSA contract administrator. It may seem like a lot of work just to be included in a group of suppliers for the federal government and not be guaranteed any contracts. However, the fact that you were certified on GSA schedule means you provide a service or product that meets the high standards of the U.S. Government. You are now able to procure a bid under the schedule, however, it's essential to continually follow-up and market your services. Public sector opportunities are no different than private sector; winning federal contracts requires diligence, best practices in business, best value, and a high standard of customer service.

Increase visibility

With the proper strategy, working for government clients will enhance how private-sector clients see your business. For our firm, it has meant greater national recognition.

Increase staff

Government business will create both a work and revenue stream which will allow your business to grow. You will be able to hire more staff and also acquire a wider range of qualified employees by applicants knowing you are registered and certified to do work for the government.

Broaden range of clientele

The combination of increased visibility and increased capability resulting from staff growth will allow you to broaden your private sector clientele. Being a recognized government supplier also opens the door to networking opportunities and industry partnerships that further increase your business.

Overcome geographic barriers

As a government supplier you are no longer restricted to or by your locality. You will also connect with large corporations who are prime contractors and look to subcontract with small business.

In summary, you need to make the decision to move ahead and continue moving ahead. Never give up and seek as much assistance as possible. As an overview, the following is a quick hit list of the steps you need to take in obtaining federal contracts.

Decide to "go for it"

The most important decision to make is to go after the opportunity. Once you move forward, keep moving.

Do the work

Certification requires a great deal of work. Make sure you follow through.

Market, market, market

Certification comes with no guarantees. You need to promote yourself tirelessly. When it comes to contract acquisition, the old saying "the squeaky wheel gets the grease" is true.

Know your resources

There are a number of organizations available to help you. Take full advantage of the assistance they can provide

Follow through

Following through is a continual process. Don't rest after the first contract, or the 10th, or the 100th. Your business can always reach greater heights. Once you have achieved a goal, move ahead to achieve another. Continue to set these goals.

Take it slow, be patient, be thorough, be knowledgeable, be persistent, be informed…

…and you will be successful.
Best of luck to you in your endeavors,

Daisy Gallagher

Top Reasons to
Contract with the Government

❧

1. The government is the largest buyer in the U.S.

2. The government purchases and needs various types of products.

3. The government buys over $200 billion annually.

4. The government can be a reliable source of business.

5. The government can be a continuous source of business.

6. The government will never go out of business.

7. The government is sensitive to diversity for their contractors.

8. The government has an abundant amount of free resources to help you in your business.

9. The government introduces you to best practices.

10. The government gives you opportunities no matter where your business is located.

"At the end of the day - it feels great to be part of a special initiative which ultimately comes back to help all of us."

Table of Contents

1

1 - 33

Government Terms

Government Agencies

Government Acronyms

Government Terms, Agencies, and Acronyms

AAC: Agency Address Code

AACC: Army Atlanta Contracting Center

ACA: Army Contracting Agency

ACO: Administration Contracting Officer

ACSS: Acquisition Center for Support Services

ACT: Accounting Control Transaction

Allowances: Amounts included in the budget to cover possible additional expenditures for statutory pay increases and other requirements.

AGE: Agency Government Estimate

Americans with Disabilities Act of 1990 (ADA): Applied portions of the 1964 Civil Rights Act to the handicapped, resulting in lawsuits and institutional expenditures to increase access for the disabled.

Antitrust Policy: Collection of national and state laws (including the Sherman Antitrust Act of 1890) aimed at preventing a single business from gaining monopoly control over a particular sector of the economy.

ATF: Bureau of Alcohol, Tobacco, Firearms, and Explosives

BAA: Broad Agency Announcement

BAFO: Best and Final Offer

BAP: Business Action Plans

Basic Ordering Agreement (BOA): A general outline of the supplies or services to be provided by the contractor.

BCA: Business Case Analysis

BCI: Business Cycle Indicators

BIC: Business Information Center

Bid Opening Date (BOD): The final date that a bid must be received by the appropriate government office.

Blanket Purchase Agreement (BPA): An agreement between the government and a vendor. The agreement gives the government the option to purchase goods or services from the vendor when needed on an on-call basis.

Block Grants: A type of grant in which the donor government may structure and design an intergovernmental program for a variety of purposes with borrowed money.

Borrowing Authority: Statutory authority that permits a federal agency to incur obligations and make payments for specified purposes with borrowed money.

BRAC: Base Realignment And Closures

Broad Agency Announcement: A notice from the government that requests scientific or research proposals from private firms concerning certain areas of interest to the government. The proposals submitted by the private firms may lead to contracts.

BTS: Bureau of Transportation Statistics

Bureau of Labor Statistics: An organization in the U.S. Department of Labor.

BY: Budget Year

CAAS: Contractor Advisory and Assistance Services

CAF: Contract Access Fee

CAGE: Commercial and Government Entity Code

CAsI: Contractor Assessment Initiative

CAV: Contractor Assistance Visit

CBD: Commerce Business Daily

CBO: Congressional Budget Office

CPFF: Cost Plus Fixed-Fee

CCR: Central Contractor Registration

CDRL: Contract Data Requirements List

CEPT: Conference European des Poste et Telecommunications

CFR: Code of Federal Regulations

CLIN: Contract Line Item Number

CNT: Contract

CO: Contracting Officer

COB: Close Of Business

Code of Federal Regulations: A collection of publications that contains regulations for all Federal Departments and Agencies.

Commercial and Government Entity Code: An identification code assigned to the awardees of DOD contracts. The codes are used by DOD for record keeping purposes. Offerors do not need a CAGE code to submit a bid for a contract.

Competition in Contracting Act: A law that requires full and open competition for Federal contracts.

Concern: A qualified HUBZone small business

Controllable Budget Items: In federal budgeting this refers to programs for which the budget authority or outlays during a fiscal year can be controlled without changing existing, substantive law. The concept "relatively uncontrollable under current law" includes outlays for open-ended programs and fixed costs such as interest on the public debt, Social Security benefits, veterans' benefits and outlays to liquidate prior-year obligations. More and more spending for federal programs has become uncontrollable or relatively uncontrollable.

CONUS: Continental United States

COR: Contracting Officer Representative

Corps of Engineers (COE): An organization in the U.S. Department of the Army.

CORS: Contracting Officer Review Session

CPI: Consumer Price Index

CR: Client Representative

CRR: Cost Recovery Report

CSD: Customer Service Directors

CSO: Competitive Sourcing Official

CTAs: Contractor Teaming Arrangements

Current Services Estimates: Estimated budget authority and outlays for federal programs and operations for the forthcoming fiscal year based on continuation of existing levels of service without policy changes. The president transmits these estimates of budget authority and outlays to Congress, accompanied by the underlying economic and policy assumptions upon which they are based, when the budget is submitted.

DARO: Days After Receipt of Order

DAU: Defense Acquisition University

DDN: Defense Data Network

Defense Construction Supply Center: An organization in the U.S. Department of Defense.

Defense Electronics Supply Center: An organization in the U.S. Department of Defense, Defense Logistics Agency.

Defense Federal Acquisition Regulations (DFAR): Procurement regulations used by organizations in the Department of Defense. Also called Defense Acquisition Regulations (DAR).

Defense General Supply Center (DGSC): An organization in the U.S. Department of Defense, Defense Logistics Agency.

Defense Industrial Supply Center (DISC): An organization in the U.S. Department of Defense, Defense Logistics Agency.

DEL: Delivery

DHS: Department of Homeland Security

DIA: Defense Intelligence Agency

DISA: Defense Information Systems Agency

DLA: Defense Logistics Agency

DOD: U.S. Department of Defense

DODEA: Department Of Defense Education Activity

DOE: Department Of Energy

DOL: Department Of Labor

DOT: Department Of Transportation

DSN: Defense Switched Network

DSS: Defense Security Service

DTD: Dated

EDA: Economic Development Administration

EDI: Electronic Data (or Document) Interchange

EEOC: Equal Employment Opportunity Commission

Electronic Data (or Document) Interchange: Electronic exchange of information, paperless office.

Ethnicity: Group of people that can be identified within a larger culture or society on the basis of such factors as religion, ancestry, or language.

EO: Executive Order

EPA: Environmental Protection Agency

ERP: Enterprise Resource Planning

ESPC: Energy Savings Performance Contract

ESRS: Electronic Subcontracting Reporting System

FA: Functional Area

FAA: Federal Aviation Administration

FAIR: Federal Activities Inventory Reform

FAO: Food and Agriculture Organization

FASA: Federal Acquisition Streamlining Act

FAST: Flexible Acquisition and Sustainment Tool

FBI: Federal Bureau of Investigation

FCC: Federal Communications Commission

FDA: Food and Drug Administration

FDIC: Federal Deposit Insurance Corporation

Federal Acquisition Regulation (FAR): Procurement regulations used by both civilian and defense organizations.

FedJob: Federal Job Listing Reserve

FHWA: Federal Highway Administration

FICA: Federal Insurance Contribution Act

First Article Testing: When DOD buys certain goods they may perform extensive tests on the first item delivered.

Firm Fixed Price (FFP): A type of contract under which the government agrees to purchase goods or services at a set price.

Federally Funded Research & Development Center (FFRDC): A facility funded by the government that conducts research and development work. The facility is operated by a university or a related non-profit organization.

Federal Information Management Resources Regulation: Government-wide regulations that govern the purchase of computer goods and services.

Federal Stock Number: A code number used to identify documents sold by the U.S. Government Printing Office, Superintendent of Documents.

Federal Supply Classification: A code number used by the government to identify various items of equipment which are purchased by the government.

Federal Supply Service: An organization in the U.S. General Services Administration.

FMS: Foreign Military Sales

FOIA: Freedom Of Information Act

FPC: Federal Prime Contractor

FPDS: Federal Procurement Data System

FR: Federal Register

FRB: Federal Reserve Board

FSC: Federal Supply Classification

FSN: Federal Stock Number

FSS: Federal Supply Service

FTE: Full-Time Equivalent

FTS: Federal Technology Service

FWS: Federal Wage System

GAO: Government Accountability Office, was the General Accounting Office

GATT: General Agreement on Tariffs and Trade

GDP: Gross Domestic Product

GFE: Government-Furnished Equipment

GFI: Government-Furnished Information

GFM: Government-Furnished Materials

GFP: Government-Furnished Property

GFPR: Guaranteed Fixed Price Remediation

GIS: Geographic Information Systems

GNP: Gross National Product

GOCO: Government-Owned, Contractor Operated

GPO: Government Printing Office

GPS: Global Positioning System

GS: General Schedule

GSA: General Services Administration

GSAM: General Services Acquisition Manual

GSAR: General Services Acquisition Regulation

GWAC: Government Wide Acquisition Contracts

HHS: Department of Health and Human Services

HRA: Human Resource Advisor

HRSA: Health Resources and Services Administration

HUD: Department of Housing and Urban Development

IAW: In Accordance With

IDIQ: Indefinite Date Indefinite Quantity

IEA: International Energy Agency

IFF: Industrial Funding Fee

IGC: Industry Government Council

IGCE: Independent Government Cost Estimate

IGO: Intergovernmental Organization

IMA: Army Installation Management Agency

IMF: International Monetary Fund

Invitation for Bid (IFB): A solicitation issued by the government to prospective bidders. An IFB describes what the government requires and how the offerors will be evaluated. Award is based on the lowest bid. Negotiations are not conducted.

IRS: Internal Revenue Service

ISO: International Organization for Standardization

IT: Information Technology

ITA: International Trade Administration

ITM: IT Manager

ITR: IT Representative

ITSS: IT Solutions Shop

JAG: Judge Advocate General

JCS: Joint Cheifs of Staff

JWOD: Javits-Wagner-O'Day

KO: Government Contracting Officer

Labor Surplus Area: A Federal program to set-aside certain contracts to businesses located in areas with high unemployment.

LOC: Library Of Congress

LOCIS: Library Of Congress Information System

LSA: Labor Surplus Area

MAIDIQ: Multiple Award Indefinite-Delivery Indefinite-Quantity

MARAD: Maritime Administration

MARC: Multiple Award Remediation Contracts

MAS: Multiple Award Schedule

MBDA: Minority Business Development Agency

MDA: Missile Defense Agency

MEO: Most Efficient Organization

NAFTA: North American Free Trade Agreement

NAICS: North American Industry Codes

NARA: National Archives and Record Administration

National Stock Number: A unique number assigned by the General Services Administration which catalogs a wide range of items by commodity, group, and class.

NCMA: National Contract Management Association

NDIA: National Defense Industrial Association

NGO: Non-Governmental Organization

NHTSA: National Highway Traffic Safety Administration

NIH: National Institute of Health

NIST: National Institute of Standards and Technology

NLM: National Library of Medicine

NLT: No Later Than

NOAA: National Oceanic and Atmospheric Administration

NPS: National Park Service

NRC: Nuclear Regulatory Commission

NSNA: No Stock Number Assigned

NTSB: National Transportation Safety Board

NWS: National Weather Service, U.S. Department of Commerce

O/A: On or About

Obligations: Orders placed, contracts awarded, services received and similar transactions during a given period that will require payments during the same or future period. Such amounts include outlays for which obligations had not been previously recorded and reflect adjustments for differences between obligations previously recorded and actual outlays to liquidate those obligations.

ODC: Other Direct Cost

Official Title: Statement of a measure's subject and purpose, which appears before the enacting clause.

OGA: Other Government Agency

OICC: Officer In Charge of Construction

OJP: Office of Justice Programs

OMB: Office of Management and Budget

OPEC: Organization of Petroleum Exporting Countries

OPI: Office of Performance Improvement

OPM: Office of Personnel Management

Organization of American States: An international governmental organization formed by the states of North and South America for the protection of mutual security and interests.

OSD: Office of the Secretary of Defense

OSDBU: Office of Small and Disadvantaged Business Utilization

OSHA: Occupational Safety and Health Administration

OSP: Order Selection Process

PALT: Procurement Acquisition Lead Time

PBS: Public Building Service

PBSA: Performance Based Service Acquisitions

PL: Public Law

PMT: Performance Management Tool

P/N: Part Number

PO: Purchase Order

POC: Point Of Contact

PPIRS: Past Performance Information Retrieval System

PRAC: Pre-placed Remedial Action Contracts

Pre-Invitation Notice (PIN): A summary of a solicitation package sent to prospective bidders, who may then request the entire solicitation package.

PTAC: Procurement Technical Assistance Center

PTO: Patent and Trademark Office

PWA: Performance Work Agreement

PWS: Performance Work Statement

QASP: Quality Assurance Surveillance Plan

R&D: Research and Development

RD: Requirements Document

Red Tape: Complications and paperwork imposed on government agencies to ensure that their actions conform to the intent of a law.

Regulation: Rules placed by the federal government on how industries operate.

Regulatory Commissions: Federal agencies with responsibility in specific areas of policy.

Regulatory Policy: The policy setting governmental regulations.

Request for Proposal (RFP): A solicitation issued by the government to prospective offerors. An RFP describes what the government requires and how the offerors will be evaluated. Negotiations may be conducted with offers. Award is based on a combination of lowest price and technical merit.

Request for Quotation (RFQ): A request for market information by the government, used for planning purposes.

Revenues: Taxes, fees, gifts, and other income received by the federal government.

RFI: Request For Information

SAP: Strategic and Action Plans

SBA: Small Business Administration

SCA: Service Contract Act

SCF: Standard Competition Form

SEC: Security and Exchange Commission

SF: Standard Form

SIN: Special Item Number

SIP: Schedule Input Program

SLCF: Streamlined Competition Form

Small Business Set Aside (SBSA): A solicitation restricted to competition completed only among small businesses.

Small And Disadvantaged Business (SDB): A small business that is owned and operated by a socially or economically disadvantaged individual.

Spending Authority: The 1974 budget act defines authority as borrowing authority, contract authority, and entitlement authority for which budget authority is not provided in advance by appropriations acts.

SRD: Selection Recommendation Document

SSA: Social Security Administration

SSEB: Source Selection Evaluation Board

Standard Industrial Classification (SIC): A code number used by the government to classify goods or services by their principal purpose.

STAR: Strategic Targeted Evaluation Board

Solicitation (SOL): A document that describes the specifications of what the government requires. A solicitation is usually an IFB or a RFP.

SOO: Statement of Objectives

Statement of Work (SOW): A description of the government's requirements for purchasing a good or service

Subsidy: An economic benefit given by the government to an individual, business or group that engages in behavior deemed beneficial by policy makers. Subsidy payments can take the form of direct cash payments, tax credits or tax deductions.

TCO: Total Cost of Ownership

TM: Task Monitor

TO: Task Order

Trade Associations: Economic interest groups that represent an entire industry.

TTB: Alcohol and Tobacco Tax and Trade Bureau

UN: United Nations

United States Code (U.S.C.): A consolidation and codification of the general and permanent laws of the United States arranged by subject under 50 titles, the first six dealing with general or political subjects, and the other 44 alphabetically arranged from agriculture to war. The U.S Code is updated annually, and a new set of bound volumes is published every six years.

USA: United States Army

USACE: United States Army Corps of Engineers

USAF: United States Air Force

USDA: United States Department of Agriculture

USDOC: United States Department Of Commerce

USGS: United States Geological Survey

USMC: United States Marine Corps

USMS: United States Marshall Service

VA: Department of Veterans Affairs

VERA: Voluntary Early Retirement Authority

VETS: Veterans' Employment and Training Service

VSIP: Voluntary Separation Incentive Pay

WBC: Women's Business Center, Small Business Administration

WHO: World Health Organization

World Trade Organization (WTO): Used by the United States to open foreign markets to American goods and protect American patents abroad.

Zoning: Dividing a community into zones for different types of uses, such as business, residential subdivisions and agriculture.

Government Agencies

- 9-11 Commission (National Commission on Terrorist Attacks Upon the United States)
- Administration for Children and Families (ACF)
- Administration for Native Americans
- Administration on Aging (AoA)
- Administration on Developmental Disabilities
- Administrative Committee of the Federal Register
- Administrative Office of the U.S. Courts
- Advisory Council on Historic Preservation
- African Development Foundation
- Agency for Healthcare Research and Quality (AHRQ)
- Agency for International Development
- Agency for Toxic Substances and Disease Registry
- Agricultural Marketing Service
- Agricultural Research Service
- Agriculture Department (USDA)
- Air Force
- Alabama Home Page
- Alabama State, County and City Websites
- Alaska Home Page
- Alaska State, County and City Websites
- Alcohol and Tobacco Tax and Trade Bureau (Treasury)
- Alcohol, Tobacco, Firearms, and Explosives Bureau (Justice)
- American Battle Monuments Commission
- American Forces Information Service
- American Samoa Home Page
- AMTRAK (National Railroad Passenger Corporation)
- Animal and Plant Health Inspection Service
- Appalachian Regional Commission
- Architect of the Capitol
- Architectural and Transportation Barriers Compliance Board (Access Board)
- Archives (National Archives and Records Administration)

- Arctic Research Commission
- Arizona Home Page
- Arizona State, County and City Websites
- Arkansas Home Page
- Arkansas State, County and City Web sites
- Armed Forces Retirement Home
- Arms Control and International Security
- Army
- Army Corps of Engineers
- Arthritis and Musculoskeletal Interagency Coordinating Committee
- Atlantic Fleet Forces Command
- Bankruptcy Courts
- Barry M. Goldwater Scholarship and Excellence in Education Foundation
- Botanic Garden
- Broadcasting Board of Governors (Voice of America, Radio/TV Marti and more)
- Bureau of Alcohol and Tobacco Tax and Trade (Treasury)
- Bureau of Alcohol, Tobacco, Firearms, and Explosives (Justice)
- Bureau of Citizenship and Immigration Services (DHS)
- Bureau of Economic Analysis (BEA)
- Bureau of Engraving and Printing
- Bureau of Indian Affairs (BIA)
- Bureau of Industry and Security (formerly the Bureau of Export Administration)
- Bureau of International Labor Affairs
- Bureau of Justice Statistics
- Bureau of Labor Statistics
- Bureau of Land Management (BLM)
- Bureau of Prisons
- Bureau of Public Debt
- Bureau of Reclamation
- Bureau of the Census
- Bureau of Transportation Statistics
- California Home Page

- California State, County and City Web sites
- Census Bureau
- Center for Nutrition Policy and Promotion
- Centers for Disease Control and Prevention (CDC)
- Centers for Medicare & Medicaid Services (formerly the Health Care Financing Administration)
- Central Command (CENTCOM)
- Central Intelligence Agency (CIA)
- Chemical Safety and Hazard Investigation Board
- Chief Financial Officers Council
- Chief Information Officers Council
- Cities, Counties, and Towns in the United States
- Citizens' Health Care Working Group
- Citizens' Stamp Advisory Committee
- Citizenship and Immigration Services Bureau (formerly Immigration and Naturalization Service)
- Civilian Radioactive Waste Management
- Coalition Provisional Authority (in Iraq)
- Coast Guard
- Colorado Home Page
- Colorado State, County and City Web sites
- Commerce Department
- Commission of Fine Arts
- Commission on Civil Rights
- Commission on International Religious Freedom
- Commission on Review of Overseas Military Facility Structure of the United States (Overseas Basing Commission)
- Commission on Security and Cooperation in Europe (Helsinki Commission)
- Commission on the Intelligence Capabilities of the United States Regarding Weapons of Mass Destruction
- Committee for Purchase from People Who Are Blind or Severely Disabled
- Committee for the Implementation of Textile Agreements
- Committee on Foreign Investments in the United States
- Commodity Futures Trading Commission

- Community Development Office (Agriculture Department)
- Community Oriented Policing Services (COPS)
- Community Planning and Development
- Comptroller of the Currency Office
- Computer Emergency Readiness Team (US CERT)
- Congressional Budget Office (CBO)
- Connecticut Home Page
- Connecticut State, County and City Web sites
- Constitution Center
- Consumer Product Safety Commission (CPSC)
- Cooperative State Research, Education and Extension Service
- Coordinating Council on Juvenile Justice and Delinquency Prevention
- Copyright Office (Library of Congress)
- Corporation for National and Community Service
- Corps of Engineers
- Council of Economic Advisers
- Council on Environmental Quality
- County and City Governments
- Court of Appeals for the Armed Forces
- Court of Appeals for the Federal Circuit
- Court of Appeals for Veterans Claims
- Court of Federal Claims
- Court of International Trade
- Court Services and Offender Supervision Agency for the District of Columbia
- Customs and Border Protection
- Defense Acquisition University
- Defense Advanced Research Projects Agency (DARPA)
- Defense Commissary Agency
- Defense Contract Audit Agency (DCAA)
- Defense Contract Management Agency
- Defense Department (DOD)
- Defense Field Activities
- Defense Finance and Accounting Service (DFAS)

- Defense Information Systems Agency (DISA)
- Defense Intelligence Agency (DIA)
- Defense Legal Services Agency
- Defense Logistics Agency (DLA)
- Defense Nuclear Facilities Safety Board
- Defense Security Cooperation Agency (DSCA)
- Defense Security Service (DSS)
- Defense Technical Information Center
- Defense Threat Reduction Agency (DTRA)
- Delaware Home Page
- Delaware River Basin Commission
- Delaware State, County and City Web sites
- Denali Commission
- Department of Agriculture (USDA)
- Department of Commerce (DOC)
- Department of Defense (DOD)
- Department of Defense Inspector General
- Department of Education (ED)
- Department of Energy (DOE)
- Department of Health and Human Services (HHS)
- Department of Homeland Security (DHS)
- Department of Housing and Urban Development (HUD)
- Department of Justice (DOJ)
- Department of Labor (DOL)
- Department of State (DOS)
- Department of the Interior (DOI)
- Department of the Treasury
- Department of Transportation (DOT)
- Department of Veterans Affairs (VA)
- Director of National Intelligence
- Disability Employment Policy Office
- District of Columbia Home Page
- Domestic Policy Council
- Drug Enforcement Administration (DEA)
- Economic Adjustment Office

- Economic Analysis, Bureau of
- Economic and Statistics Administration
- Economic Development Administration
- Economic Research Service
- Economic, Business and Agricultural Affairs (State Department)
- Education Department (ED)
- Election Assistance Commission
- Elementary and Secondary Education
- Employee Benefits Security Administration (formerly Pension and Welfare Benefits Administration)
- Employment and Training Administration (Labor Department)
- Employment Standards Administration
- Endangered Species Committee
- Energy Department (DOE)
- Energy Efficiency and Renewable Energy
- Energy Information Administration
- Enforcement (Treasury Department)
- English Language Acquisition Office
- Engraving and Printing, Bureau of
- Environment, Safety and Health
- Environmental Management (Energy Department)
- Environmental Protection Agency (EPA)
- Equal Employment Opportunity Commission (EEOC)
- European Command
- Executive Office for Immigration Review
- Export Administration (now the Bureau of Industry and Security)
- Export-Import Bank of the United States
- Fair Housing and Equal Opportunity
- Faith-Based and Community Initiatives Office
- Farm Credit Administration
- Farm Service Agency
- Federal Accounting Standards Advisory Board
- Federal Aviation Administration (FAA)
- Federal Bureau of Investigation (FBI)

- Federal Bureau of Prisons
- Federal Citizen Information Center (FCIC)
- Federal Communications Commission (FCC)
- Federal Consulting Group
- Federal Deposit Insurance Corporation (FDIC)
- Federal Election Commission
- Federal Emergency Management Agency (FEMA)
- Federal Energy Regulatory Commission
- Federal Executive Boards
- Federal Financial Institutions Examination Council
- Federal Highway Administration
- Federal Housing Enterprise Oversight
- Federal Housing Finance Board
- Federal Interagency Committee for the Management of Noxious and Exotic Weeds
- Federal Interagency Committee on Education
- Federal Interagency Council on Statistical Policy
- Federal Judicial Center
- Federal Labor Relations Authority
- Federal Laboratory Consortium for Technology Transfer
- Federal Law Enforcement Training Center
- Federal Library and Information Center Committee
- Federal Maritime Commission
- Federal Mediation and Conciliation Service
- Federal Mine Safety and Health Review Commission
- Federal Motor Carrier Safety Administration
- Federal Railroad Administration
- Federal Reserve System
- Federal Retirement Thrift Investment Board
- Federal Student Aid
- Federal Trade Commission (FTC)
- Federal Transit Administration
- Federated States of Micronesia Home Page
- Financial Management Service (Treasury Department)
- Fish and Wildlife Service

- Florida Home Page
- Florida State, County and City Web sites
- Food and Drug Administration (FDA)
- Food and Nutrition Service
- Food Safety and Inspection Service
- Food, Nutrition and Consumer Services
- Foreign Agricultural Service
- Foreign Claims Settlement Commission
- Forest Service
- Fossil Energy
- Fulbright Foreign Scholarship Board
- General Services Administration (GSA)
- Geological Survey (USGS)
- Georgia Home Page
- Georgia State, County and City Web sites
- Global Affairs (State Department)
- Global Communications Office (White House)
- Government Accountability Office (GAO)
- Government National Mortgage Association
- Government Printing Office (GPO)
- Grain Inspection, Packers and Stockyards Administration
- Guam Home Page
- Harry S. Truman Scholarship Foundation
- Hawaii Home Page
- Hawaii State, County and City Web sites
- Health and Human Services Department (HHS)
- Health Resources and Services Administration
- Helsinki Commission (Commission on Security and Cooperation in Europe)
- Holocaust Memorial Museum
- Homeland Security Department (DHS)
- House Leadership Offices
- House of Representatives
- House of Representatives Committees
- House Office of Inspector General

- House Office of the Clerk
- House Organizations, Commissions, and Task Forces
- House Representatives on the Web
- Housing and Urban Development Department (HUD)
- Housing Office (HUD)
- Idaho Home Page
- Idaho State, County and City Web sites
- Illinois and Michigan Canal National Heritage Corridor Commission
- Illinois Home Page
- Illinois State, County and City Web sites
- Immigration and Customs Enforcement
- Immigration and Naturalization Service (Bureau of Citizenship and Immigration Services)
- Indian Affairs, Bureau of
- Indian Arts and Crafts Board
- Indian Health Service
- Indiana Home Page
- Indiana State, County and City Web sites
- Industrial College of the Armed Forces
- Industry and Security, Bureau of (formerly the Bureau of Export Administration)
- Information Resource Management College
- Innovation and Improvement Office
- Institute of Education Sciences
- Institute of Museum and Library Services
- Institute of Peace
- Inter-American Foundation
- Interagency Alternative Dispute Resolution Working Group
- Interagency Council on Homelessness
- Interior Department
- Internal Revenue Service (IRS)
- International Broadcasting Bureau (IBB)
- International Labor Affairs, Bureau of
- International Trade Administration (ITA)

- Iowa Home Page
- Iowa State, County and City Web sites
- James Madison Memorial Fellowship Foundation
- Japan-United States Friendship Commission
- John F. Kennedy Center for the Performing Arts
- Joint Board for the Enrollment of Actuaries
- Joint Chiefs of Staff
- Joint Congressional Committee on Inaugural Ceremonies
- Joint Forces Command
- Joint Forces Staff College
- Joint Military Intelligence College
- Judicial Circuit Courts of Appeal, by Geographic Location and Circuit
- Judicial Panel on Multidistrict Litigation
- Justice Department
- Justice Programs Office (Juvenile Justice, Victims of Crime, Violence Against Women and more)
- Justice Statistics, Bureau of
- Kansas Home Page
- Kansas State, County and City Web sites
- Kentucky Home Page
- Kentucky State, County and City Web sites
- Labor Department (DOL)
- Labor Statistics, Bureau of
- Land Management, Bureau of
- Lead Hazard Control (Housing and Urban Development Department)
- Legal Services Corporation
- Library of Congress
- Local Governments
- Louisiana Home Page
- Louisiana State, County and City Web sites
- Maine Home Page
- Maine State, County and City Web sites
- Marine Corps

- Marine Mammal Commission
- Maritime Administration
- Marketing and Regulatory Programs (Agriculture Department)
- Marshals Service
- Maryland Home Page
- Maryland State, County and City Web sites
- Massachusetts Home Page
- Massachusetts State, County and City Web sites
- Medicare Payment Advisory Commission
- Merit Systems Protection Board
- Michigan Home Page
- Michigan State, County and City Web sites
- Migratory Bird Conservation Commission
- Military Postal Service Agency
- Millennium Challenge Corporation
- Mine Safety and Health Administration
- Minerals Management Service
- Minnesota Home Page
- Minnesota State, County and City Web sites
- Minority Business Development Agency
- Mint (Treasury Department)
- Missile Defense Agency (MDA)
- Mississippi Home Page
- Mississippi River Commission
- Mississippi State, County and City Web sites
- Missouri Home Page
- Missouri State, County and City Web sites
- Montana Home Page
- Montana State, County and City Web sites
- Morris K. Udall Foundation: Scholarship and Excellence in National Environmental Policy
- Multifamily Housing Office
- National Aeronautics and Space Administration (NASA)
- National Agricultural Statistics Service
- National AIDS Policy Office

- National Archives and Records Administration (NARA)
- National Bipartisan Commission on the Future of Medicare
- National Capital Planning Commission
- National Cemetery Administration (Veterans Affairs Department)
- National Commission on Libraries and Information Science
- National Commission on Terrorist Attacks Upon the United States (9-11 Commission)
- National Constitution Center
- National Council on Disability
- National Counterintelligence Executive, Office of
- National Credit Union Administration
- National Defense University
- National Drug Intelligence Center
- National Economic Council
- National Endowment for the Arts
- National Endowment for the Humanities
- National Gallery of Art
- National Geospatial-Intelligence Agency
- National Guard
- National Highway Traffic Safety Administration
- National Indian Gaming Commission
- National Institute of Justice
- National Institute of Standards and Technology (NIST)
- National Institutes of Health (NIH)
- National Interagency Fire Center
- National Labor Relations Board
- National Laboratories (Energy Department)
- National Marine Fisheries
- National Mediation Board
- National Nuclear Security Administration
- National Ocean Service
- National Oceanic and Atmospheric Administration (NOAA)
- National Park Foundation
- National Park Service

- National Railroad Passenger Corporation (AMTRAK)
- National Reconnaissance Office
- National Science Foundation
- National Security Agency (NSA)
- National Security Council
- National Technical Information Service
- National Telecommunications and Information Administration
- National Transportation Safety Board
- National War College
- National Weather Service
- Natural Resources Conservation Service
- Navy
- Nebraska Home Page
- Nebraska State, County and City Web sites
- Nevada Home Page
- Nevada State, County and City Web sites
- New Hampshire Home Page
- New Hampshire State, County and City Web sites
- New Jersey Home Page
- New Jersey State, County and City Web sites
- New Mexico Home Page
- New Mexico State, County and City Web sites
- New York Home Page
- New York State, County and City Web sites
- North Carolina Home Page
- North Carolina State, County and City Web sites
- North Dakota Home Page
- North Dakota State, County and City Web sites
- Northern Command
- Northwest Power Planning Council
- Nuclear Energy, Science and Technology
- Nuclear Regulatory Commission
- Nuclear Waste Technical Review Board
- Oak Ridge National Laboratory
- Occupational Safety & Health Administration (OSHA)

- Occupational Safety and Health Review Commission
- Office of Compliance
- Office of Federal Housing Enterprise Oversight
- Office of Government Ethics
- Office of Management and Budget (OMB)
- Office of National Drug Control Policy (ONDCP)
- Office of Personnel Management
- Office of Refugee Resettlement
- Office of Science and Technology Policy
- Office of Scientific and Technical Information
- Office of Special Counsel
- Office of Thrift Supervision
- Ohio Home Page
- Ohio State, County and City Web sites
- Oklahoma Home Page
- Oklahoma State, County and City Web sites
- Oregon Home Page
- Oregon State, County and City Web sites
- Overseas Basing Commission (Commission on Review of
- Overseas Military Facility Structure of the United States)
- Overseas Private Investment Corporation
- Pacific Command
- Pardon Attorney Office
- Parole Commission (Justice Department)
- Patent and Trademark Office
- Peace Corps
- Pennsylvania Home Page
- Pennsylvania State, County and City Web sites
- Pension and Welfare Benefits Administration (now the Employee Benefits Security Administration)
- Pension Benefit Guaranty Corporation
- Pentagon Force Protection Agency
- Pipeline and Hazardous Materials Safety Administration
- Policy Development and Research (Housing and Urban Development Department)

- Political Affairs (State Department)
- Postal Rate Commission
- Postal Service (USPS)
- Postsecondary Education
- Power Administrations
- President's Commission on Moon, Mars and Beyond
- President's Commission on the U.S. Postal Service
- President's Council on Integrity and Efficiency
- President's Foreign Intelligence Advisory Board
- Presidio Trust
- Prisoner of War/Missing Personnel Office
- Public and Indian Housing
- Public Debt, Bureau of
- Public Diplomacy and Public Affairs (State Department)
- Puerto Rico Home Page
- Radio and TV Marti (Español)
- Radio Free Asia (RFA)
- Radio Free Europe/Radio Liberty (RFE/RL)
- Railroad Retirement Board
- Reclamation, Bureau of
- Refugee Resettlement
- Regulatory Information Service Center
- Rehabilitation Services Administration (Education Department)
- Research and Innovative Technology Administration (Transportation Department)
- Research, Education and Economics (Agriculture Department)
- Rhode Island Home Page
- Rhode Island State, County and City Web sites
- Risk Management Agency (Agriculture Department)
- Rural Business-Cooperative Service
- Rural Development
- Rural Housing Service
- Rural Utilities Service
- Saint Lawrence Seaway Development Corporation
- Science Office (Energy Department)

- Secret Service
- Securities and Exchange Commission (SEC)
- Selective Service System
- Senate
- Senate Committees
- Senate Leadership
- Senators on the Web
- Small Business Administration (SBA)
- Smithsonian Institution
- Social Security Administration (SSA)
- Social Security Advisory Board
- South Carolina Home Page
- South Carolina State, County and City Web sites
- South Dakota Home Page
- South Dakota State, County and City Web sites
- Southern Command
- Special Education and Rehabilitative Services
- Special Forces Operations Command
- State Agencies by Topic
- State Department
- State Home Pages
- State Justice Institute
- Stennis Center for Public Service
- Strategic Command
- Substance Abuse and Mental Health Services Administration
- Superfund Basic Research Program
- Supreme Court of the United States
- Surface Mining, Reclamation and Enforcement
- Surface Transportation Board
- Susquehanna River Basin Commission
- Tax Court
- Taxpayer Advocacy Panel
- Technology Administration
- Tennessee Home Page
- Tennessee State, County and City Web sites

- Tennessee Valley Authority
- Territories of the United States
- Texas Home Page
- Texas State, County and City Web sites
- Trade and Development Agency
- Transportation Command
- Transportation Department (DOT)
- Transportation Security Administration
- Transportation Statistics, Bureau of
- Treasury Department
- TRICARE Management
- Trustee Program (Justice Department)
- U.S. Border Patrol (now Customs and Border Protection)
- U.S. Centennial of Flight Commission
- U.S. Citizenship and Immigration Services
- U.S. Customs and Border Protection
- U.S. Immigration and Customs Enforcement
- U.S. International Trade Commission
- U.S. Military Academy, West Point
- U.S. Mint
- U.S. Mission to the United Nations
- U.S. National Central Bureau - Interpol (Justice Department)
- U.S. Postal Service (USPS)
- U.S. Sentencing Commission
- U.S. Trade Representative
- U.S. Virgin Islands
- Unified Combatant Commands (Defense Department)
- Uniformed Services University of the Health Sciences
- Utah Home Page
- Utah State, County and City Web sites
- Vermont Home Page
- Vermont State, County or City Web sites
- Veterans Affairs Department (VA)
- Veterans Benefits Administration
- Veterans Day National Committee

- Veterans Health Administration
- Veterans' Employment and Training Service
- Vietnam Educational Foundation
- Virginia Home Page
- Virginia State, County and City Web sites
- Vocational and Adult Education
- Voice of America (VOA)
- Washington Headquarters Services
- Washington Home Page
- Washington State, County and City Web sites
- Weather Service, National
- West Point (Army)
- West Virginia Home Page
- West Virginia State, County and City Web sites
- White House
- White House Commission on Presidential Scholars
- White House Commission on the National Moment of Remembrance
- White House Office of Administration
- Wisconsin Home Page
- Wisconsin State, County and City Web sites
- Women's Bureau (Labor Department)
- Woodrow Wilson International Center for Scholars
- Worldnet Television
- Wyoming Home Page
- Wyoming State, County and City Web sites

Source: http://www.firstgov.gov/index.shtml

2   35 - 75   Certifications

Certification or
Qualification Requirements

❧

- To qualify as small business: a business concern eligible for assistance from SBA as a small business is one that is organized for profit, with a place of business located in the United States. It must operate primarily within the United States or make a significant contribution to the U.S. economy through payment of taxes or use of American products, materials or labor. Together with its affiliates, it must meet the numerical size standards as defined in the Small Business Size Regulations.

- SBA's size standards define whether a business entity is small and, thus, eligible for Government programs and preferences reserved for "small business" concerns. Size standards have been established for types of economic activity, or industry, generally under the North American Industry Classification System (NAICS).

- NAICS is described in the North American Industry Classification Manual-United States, which is available from the National Technical Information Service, 5285 Port Royal Road, Springfield, VA 22161; by calling 1(800) 553-6847 or 1(703) 605-6000; or via the Internet at **http://www.sba.gov/about-offices-content/1/2895**. The manual includes definitions for each industry, tables showing relationships between 1997 NAICS and 1987 SICs, and a comprehensive index. NAICS assigns codes to all economic activity within twenty broad sectors.

- The applicant firm must be a small business, must be unconditionally owned and controlled by one or more socially and economically disadvantaged individuals who are of good character and citizens of the United States, and must demonstrate potential for success.

- Mentor - Protégé Program: How does a firm enter the program? Mentor and protégé firms enter into an SBA-approved written agreement outlining the protégé's needs and describing the assistance the mentor has committed to providing. The protégé's servicing district office evaluates the agreement according to the provisions contained in 13 CFR 124.520. SBA conducts annual reviews to determine the success of the mentor-protégé relationship.

- HUBZone: To participate in the HUBZone Empowerment Contracting Program, a concern must be determined to be a "qualified HUBZone small business concern." A firm can be found to be a qualified HUBZone concern, if:
  - It is small
  - It is located in an "historically underutilized business zone" (HUBZone)
  - It is owned and controlled by one or more U.S. Citizens
  - At least 35% of its employees reside in a HUBZone

Woman-Owned Small Business

❧

Eligibility Requirements

To be eligible, a firm must be at least 51% owned and controlled by one or more women, and primarily managed by one or more women. The women must be U.S. citizens. The firm must be "small" in its primary industry in accordance with SBA's size standards for that industry. In order for a WOSB to be deemed "economically disadvantaged," its owners must demonstrate economic disadvantage in accordance with the requirements set forth in the final rule.

WOSB Program Third Party Certification – *Updated*

The SBA has approved four organizations to act as Third Party Certifiers under the WOSB Program. The four organizations and contact information are:

- El Paso Hispanic Chamber of Commerce
- National Women Business Owners Corporation
- US Women's Chamber of Commerce
- Women's Business Enterprise National Council (WBENC)

Women Owned Small Businesses may elect to use the services of a Third Party Certifier to demonstrate eligibility for the program, or they may self-certify using the process outlined here on this website. SBA will only accept third party certification from these entities, and firms are still subject to the same eligibility requirements to participate in the program.

Please note, at the request of WBENC, SBA has approved WBENC only for the certification of WOSBs and not for the certification of Economically Disadvantaged WOSBs.

Getting Started

For a quick overview of the WOSB Program and what businesses need to do to participate, click here to view a short presentation. For detailed information about the WOSB Program, see the "WOSB Program Information" section.

4 Steps to participate in the WOSB program:

1. Read the WOSB Federal Contract program regulations in the Federal Register and the WOSB Compliance Guide.
2. Register and represent your status in the System for Award Management (SAM) as WOSB or EDWOSB.**
3. Log onto SBA's General Login System (GLS). *Obtain an account now if you don't already have one*
4. Go to the WOSB program repository (through GLS) and upload / categorize all required documents.

WOSB Program Repository

To access the WOSB Program Repository, users must first login to SBA's General Login System (GLS). If you do not have an account:

- Log onto SBA's General Login System (GLS)
- Click on "Instructions for GLS" for information on how to request an account
- Go to "Request SBA User ID" to create an account

Once you are in GLS, click the "Access" button at the top of the screen. Then select "Women-Owned Small Business Program Repository" and press submit. You should then be able to access the repository. Once you are in the repository, you can click the "Help" button at the top of the screen for instructions on how to use the repository.

A complete list of required documents to upload to the Repository can be found in the Compliance Guide for the WOSB Program. All eligible WOSBs and EDWOSBs who would like to participate in this program **must complete and sign the WOSB or EDWOSB certification form below and upload it into the repository.

WOSB Certification (SBA Form 2413)
EDWOSB Certification (SBA Form 2414)

Questions about the WOSB Program?

SBA Answer Desk
1-800-U-ASK-SBA (1-800-827-5722)
Answer Desk TTY: (704) 344-6640
[Spanish]
Email: wosb@sba.gov.

In addition to our website and the SBA Answer Desk, there are a number of resources available to help answer questions about the WOSB program:

Visit a local resource:

Small Business District Offices
Find your local office at: http://www.sba.gov/about-offices-list/2

Women's Business Centers
Find your local center at: http://www.sba.gov/content/womens-business-centers

Small Business Development Centers
Find your local center at: http://www.asbdc-us.org/

Procurement Technical Assistance Centers
Find your local center at: http://www.aptac-us.org/new/

Source: *http://www.sba.gov/content/contracting-opportunities-women-owned-small-businesses*

Private, national women's business organizations that certify qualified women-owned businesses:

Women's Business Enterprise National Council (WBENC)

- Offers a comprehensive certification for women-owned businesses administered through fourteen regional affiliates and accepted by more than 400 national corporations as well as state and local government agencies.

The National Women's Business Owners Corporation (NWBOC)

- The NWBOC has launched a national certification program for women-owned and controlled businesses as an alternative to the multiple state and local certifications required by many public and private sector agencies or prime contractors.

How does the Federal Government define a "women-owned small business"?

- The Federal Acquisition Regulations (FAR) defines a "women-owned small business" as a small business concern.
- Which is at least 51% owned by one or more women; or, in the case of any publicly owned business, at least 51% of the stock of which is owned by one or more women; and
- Whose management and daily business operations are controlled by one or more women."

Source: http://www.sba.gov/GC/index-programs-cawbo.html

HUBZone Certification

❧

To be eligible for HUBZone certification you must:

- Be a small business by SBA standards
- Be located in a historically underutilized business zone
- (HUBZone)
- Be wholly owned and controlled by person(s) who are
- U.S. citizens
- Have at least 35% of its employees reside in a HUBZone

A "HUBZone" is an area that is located within one or more of the following:

- A qualified census tract
- A qualified "non-metropolitan county" with a median household income of less than 80 percent of the State median or with an unemployment rate of not less than 140 percent of the statewide average, based on US Department of Labor recent data; or
- Located within the boundaries of federally recognized Indian reservations.

Eligible HUBZone SBA concerns are able to receive several different types of contracts:

- A HUBZone set-aside contract can be awarded if the contracting officer has a reasonable expectation that at least two qualified HUBZone small businesses will submit offers and that the contract can be awarded at a fair market price.
- A sole source HUBZone contract can be awarded if the contracting officer does not have a reasonable expectation that two or more qualified HUBZone small businesses will submit

offers, determines that the qualified HUBZone small business is responsible, and determines that the contract can be awarded at a fair price. The government estimate for a HUBZone sole source contract cannot exceed $5 million for manufacturing requirements or $3 million for all other requirements.

- A full and open competition contract can be awarded with a price evaluation preference for qualified HUBZone SBCs. The offer of the HUBZone small business will be considered lower than the offer of a non-HUBZone/non-small business, provided that the offer of the HUBZone small business is not more than 10 percent higher.

To be awarded contracts under the program, your firm must first meet HUBZone eligibility requirements, be certified by the U.S. Small Business Administration (SBA) as a qualified HUBZone small business, and be listed on SBA's 'List of Qualified HUBZone SBCs' and in SBA Supplemental Page's database.

Information SBA needs to determine eligibility:

- Basic information to identify your firm and the location of its principal office, to establish whether it is located in a HUBZone.
- Information about who owns and manages your firm, to establish whether it is owned and controlled by US Citizens.
- Information about your firm's employees, to establish whether at least 35% of them reside in a HUBZone.
- Information about your firm's financial condition, to establish, track, and evaluate its progress.

To be certified as a qualified HUBZone small business concern you must submit an electronic application, and will need the following information:

- Special licenses
- If your firm is a corporation, its articles of incorporation and stockholder's register. If your firm is a partnership, its partnership agreement. If your firm is a limited liability company, its company agreement
- Financial statements for your firm's three most recently completed fiscal years. If your firm has been in operation less than three years, financial statements covering however long it has been in operation
- If it's a franchise, the franchise agreement
- A current employee roster providing employee name, home address, and date of employment
- Employment records for the past twelve months
- A listing of any Federal Employment Tax Credits the
- firm receives
- Information on any current bonding arrangements through a company or individual not formally recognized as a surety provider
- Information on any non-bank lender(s) who provides credit to the firm (should cover name and citizenship of creditor, and amount owed)
- Information (name, address, kind of business, etc.) about any other businesses that the owners, directors, or officers of your business own or manage
- Information from the birth certificate or certificate of
- naturalization for each owner, manager, member of the
- board of directors, or officer

When filing an electronic application, you must work through the application until it is fully complete, and it must be done in one single session.

Completing the HUBZone certification application (the following are important sections to be filled out):

- If you have received a SBA Customer ID and password from SBA before, you will have to enter them in order to get to the remaining sections of the HUBZone application. If you do not have an ID and a password, you must create a business profile through the SBA Supplemental Page web-site

- Packager Information: A packager is described as a business counselor, attorney, assistance center representative or similar provider that is helping the applicant firm with this application process.

- Location in a Qualified HUBZone: This information is automatically compiled based on information you supplied in SBA Supplemental Page.

- General Business Information - The answers to these questions will help us determine how to process your application most efficiently, to get in touch with you if we need to, and to analyze certain aspects of your firm's eligibility for the program.

- Ownership and Control - Your answers to these questions will help us determine whether your firm is 100% owned and controlled by U.S. citizens

- HUBZone Employment - This information will enable us to determine if at least 35% of your firm's employees reside in a HUBZone.

- Financial Information - This information will provide a basic financial profile of your firm.

- Affiliation - This information will help us determine if your firm is independently owned and operated and/or meets specific criteria for HUBZone company affiliation.

- Additional Point of Contact - The Key/Other Person who is responsible to verify and attest the application for further processing.

After you have completed the electronic version of the application, SBA's software will audit it and advise you of any incomplete or missing data. Safeguards are built into the software to prevent you from submitting an incomplete application. The system will alert you if supporting documentation is required to complete the application review.

Source: http://www.sba.gov/category/navigation-structure/contracting/working-with-government/small-business-certifications-audiences/hubzone-certification

Central Contractor Registration (CCR)
*Will be replaced by SAM**

⚜

The Central Contractor Registration system is a central repository of all companies and agencies wanting to do business with the Federal Government. These companies and agencies MUST be registered and validated in the CCR prior to award of any contract, basic agreement, basic ordering agreement, or blanket purchase agreement, unless the award results from a solicitation issued on or before May 31, 1998.

General Information:

- A DUNS number provided by Dun & Bradstreet (D&B) is required. As a result, D&B may include your basic information (i.e. company name, address) in some of their products, such as mailing lists. If at anytime you do not wish to be included in these D&B products or have questions, please contact them at 1-866-705-5711 if U.S. based or via the D&B web if non-USA.

- Non-USA registrants must also obtain a North Atlantic Treaty Organization (NATO) CAGE (NCAGE) Code.

- A CAGE Code is needed: The Commercial and Government Entity (CAGE) Code is a five-character ID number used extensively within the federal government. Vendors with a U.S. address may submit the application without a CAGE Code if they do not have one. If your application does not contain a CAGE Code, one will be assigned to you. The CCR registration process will also verify existing CAGE Codes for all applicants. To speed up the process, make every effort to use a current CAGE Code in your application. You must have a separate CAGE Code for each physical location and separate division at the same physical location. Each separate CCR registration must have its own CAGE Code. If you think you have a CAGE Code, search the DLIS CAGE web at

http://www.dlis.dla.mil/cage_welcome.asp.

NOTE: Vendors located outside of the U.S. are required to include an NCAGE Code on the registration, or it will be considered incomplete.

- Legal Business Name and Doing Business As (DBA): Enter the legal name by which you are incorporated and pay taxes. If you commonly use another name, such as a franchise or licensee name, then include that in the DBA space below the Legal Business Name. Your legal business name as entered on the CCR registration MUST match the legal business name at Dun & Bradstreet. If the information does not match, your registration may be rejected during processing. Do not type "same" or "as shown above" in the DBA field.
- US Federal TIN: The Tax Identification Number (TIN) is the nine-digit number which is either an Employer Identification Number (EIN) assigned by the Internal Revenue Service (IRS) or Social Security Number (SSN) assigned by the Social Security Administration (SSA)
- Division name and number: If you do business as a division of a larger company, then you must enter the information where needed.
- Company URL: If applicable, provide your company's homepage URL.
- Physical Street Address 1: You must include a valid street address where your business is located. If you use a PO Box for correspondence, this may be included in the space allocated for "mailing address." Your street address, as entered on the CCR registration, MUST match the street address assigned to your D&B D-U-N-S Number. If the information does not match, your registration may be rejected during processing. You may

not register a branch of the business with the branch address and the headquarters D-U-N-S Number.

- City, State, and Zip: The nine-digit zip code is mandatory. When entering the nine-digit zip code on the web, enter numbers only; do not include the dash.

- Country: Choose the appropriate country code abbreviation from the list provided.

- Mailing Address Information: If you are unable to receive mail at your physical address, enter a proper mailing address here. A Post Office Box is permissible. Any address used here will receive all CCR correspondence. If the Point of Contact is in a different location than the legal business address and wishes to receive the mail directly, please enter the appropriate address here.

- Date Business Started: Enter the date your business was started in its present form. This may be used to distinguish you from others with similar names. When entering the information on the web site, you must enter as mm/dd/yyyy.

- Fiscal Year End Close Date: Enter the day on which you close your fiscal year. When entering the information on the web site, you must enter as mm/dd.

- Average Number of Employees: Be sure to provide accurate information about the number of employees for your business, as this value is part of determining your business size classification. The calculation must include the employees of all affiliates, not just your individual branch.

- Annual Revenue: Be sure to provide accurate information about the three-year average annual revenue for your business, as this value is part of determining your business size classification. The calculation must include the revenue of all affiliates, not just your individual branch.

- Company Security Level: If applicable, choose the correct level of security for the facility.

- Highest Employee Security Level: If applicable, choose the security level of the employee with the highest employee security level at that facility.

Corporate Information

- Type of Relationship with the U.S. Federal Government:
- Contracts: This option is for those who plan to respond to federal government contracts.
- Grants: This option is for those who plan to respond to federal government grants.
- Both Contracts and Grants: This option is for those who plan to respond to both federal government contracts and grants.
- Type of Organization: You must choose one of the boxes to indicate the legal form of your business.
- Corporate Entity (Not Tax Exempt): If you choose Corporation as your status, you must enter the state of incorporation if incorporated in the U.S. If you are incorporated outside the U.S., you must provide country of incorporation and check foreign supplier under business types.
- Corporate Entity (Tax Exempt): If you choose Corporation as your status, you must enter the state of incorporation if incorporated in the U.S. If you are incorporated outside the U.S., you must provide country of incorporation and check foreign supplier under business types.
- Partnership
- Sole Proprietorship
- Owner Information: Mandatory if you have checked "Sole Proprietorship" as business type. You must provide the name and phone number of the owner of the business.

U.S. Government Entity

- Federal
- State
- Local
- Foreign Government
- International Organization: Defined in the Code of Federal Regulations

- Business Types: Check all the descriptions that apply to your business (you must choose at least one). If you are a small business, emerging small business, or a participant in SBA programs such as 8(a) and HUB Zone, this information will be inserted into your registration directly from SBA. You will not need to enter this information.

Goods / Services

- North American Industry Classification System (NAICS) Codes: NAICS Codes are a method for classifying business establishments.
- Standard Industrial Classification (SIC) Codes: Use this section to list all the classification codes that apply to your products and services.
- Product Service Codes (PSC Codes): PSC Codes are optional, four-character, and alpha-numeric. PSC Codes are similar to SIC Codes. PSC Codes are used only to identify services.
- Federal Supply Classification Codes (FSC Codes): FSC Codes are optional, 4-numeric digits. FSC Codes are similar to SIC Codes. FSC Codes are used only to identify products.

Financial Information: All registrants must complete this section except Non U.S. vendors doing business outside the U.S. and federal government agencies. Electronic Funds Transfer (EFT) is the U.S. Federal Government's preferred payment method and has been legally mandated for all contract payments.

- Financial Institution: Name of the bank used for EFT/banking purposes. This field will be automatically filled from the ABA Routing Number provided below.
- ABA Routing Number: ABA Routing number is the American Banking Association nine-digit routing transit number of your financial institution. This number must be the EFT ABA routing number, not the Wire Transfer ABA number.

- Account Number, Type, & Lockbox Number: Enter the appropriate account number to which you want your EFT payments deposited and check the proper box to indicate whether it is a checking or savings account. If you prefer to use a lockbox service, enter the appropriate account number in the space provided. If you use a lockbox for your banking purposes, you must also check "checking" under account type.

- Automated Clearing House (ACH): ACH is the Automated Clearing House department of your bank. Enter the appropriate contact information for the ACH coordinator at your bank. This information is necessary should problems occur with your EFT transfer. Payment locations must have a bank contact to call.

- ABA Routing Number: ABA Routing number is the American Banking Association nine-digit routing transit number of your financial institution. This number must be the EFT ABA routing number, not the Wire Transfer ABA number.

- Remittance Information: This is the address where you would like a paper check mailed in the event an EFT transfer does not work. Please indicate on the name line the party to whom the check should be mailed to and fill in the appropriate information. If you use a lockbox and want checks mailed directly to the bank, insert the bank name and address here.

- Accounts Receivable: Provide contact information for the accounts receivable person at your company. An e-mail address is required. This is the contact provided to Defense Finance and Accounting Service regarding EFT payments on your federal government contracts.

- Financial Information: All registrants must complete this section except Non U.S. vendors doing business outside the U.S. and federal government agencies. Electronic Funds Transfer (EFT) is the U.S. Federal Government's preferred payment method and has been legally mandated for all contract payments.

- Credit Card Information: Does your company accept credit cards for payment? This is a YES or NO question.

Point of Contact

- Registrant Name: Also known as the CCR POC. List the name of the person that acknowledges that the information provided in the registration is current, accurate, and complete. The person named here will be the ONLY person within the registering company to receive the Trading Partner Identification Number (TPIN) via e-mail or U.S. Postal mail. The Registrant and the Alternate Contact are the only people authorized to share information with CCR Assistance Center personnel. It is important that the person named here have knowledge about the CCR Registration. An e-mail address is required. Both upper and lower cases are acceptable for all e-mail addresses.
- CCR POC Alternate: Provide name and a phone number for another person at your company should questions arise when the primary contact is not available.
- Government Business POC: This POC is that person in the company responsible for marketing and sales with the federal government. An e-mail address is required. Both upper and lower cases are acceptable for all e-mail addresses. This POC and contact information, if entered, will be publicly displayed on the CCR Search Page. All contact methods are mandatory.
- Past Performance POC: This POC is that person in the company responsible for administering the company's federal government past performance reports and response efforts. An e-mail address is required. Both upper and lower cases are acceptable for all e-mail addresses. This POC and contact information is optional and, if entered, will be publicly displayed on the CCR Inquiry web site. All contact methods are mandatory.
- Electronic Business POC: The EB POC is the person in the company responsible for authorizing individual company personnel access into federal government electronic business systems [e.g., Electronic Document Access (EDA), Wide Area Workflow (WAWF)]. POC and contact information is mandatory. This information will be publicly displayed on the CCR Inquiry web site. All contact methods are mandatory.

- Marketing Partner ID (MPIN): This is a self-defined access code that will be shared with authorized partner applications [e.g., Past Performance Information Retrieval System (PPIRS), Federal Technical Data Solutions (FedTeDS) etc.]. The MPIN is used to access these other systems, and you should guard it as such. The MPIN must contain nine characters; at least one alpha and one numeric character each. It should not contain spaces or special characters.

Source: *http://www.ccr.gov/handbook.asp#information_needed.*

*The System for Award Management (**SAM**) is a free web-site which consolidates Federal procurement systems and the Catalog of Federal Domestic Assistance. Currently CCR, FedReg, ORCA and EPLS are in process of being migrated into SAM. SAM is set to replace CCR and other systems between end of **July 2012** and October 2012. Over the coming years, additional system migrations will be completed. http://www.sam.gov If you have purchased the GCRG after July 2012 and are listed on CCR or have not yet listed your company on CCR go to the sam.gov website and follow those directions as you will need to upload and or transfer your information into SAM.

https://www.sam.gov/sam/transcript/SAM_User_Guide_v1.8.pdf

8a Business Development Certification
❧

Basic requirements a concern must meet for the 8a Business Development program:

- A concern meets the basic requirements for admission to the 8a Business Development program if, it is a small business, unconditionally owned, and controlled by one or more socially and economically disadvantaged individuals of good character and citizens of the United States, and which demonstrates potential for success.

Who is considered socially disadvantaged:

- Socially disadvantaged individuals are those who have been subjected to racial or ethnic prejudice or cultural bias within American society because of their identities as members of groups and without regard to their individual qualities. The social disadvantage must stem from circumstances beyond their control.

The following individuals have a reputable presumption of being socially disadvantaged:

- Black Americans, Hispanic Americans, Native Americans, Asian Pacific Americans, Subcontinent Asian Americans, and members of other groups designated from time to time by SBA according to procedures.
- An individual must demonstrate that he or she has held him or herself out, and is currently identified by others as a member of a designated group, if the Small Business Administration requires it.

Evidence of individual social disadvantage must include the following elements:

- At least one objective distinguishing feature that has contributed to social disadvantage, such as: race, ethnic origin, gender, physical handicap, long-term residence in an environment isolated from the mainstream of American society, or other similar causes not common to individuals who are not socially disadvantaged.
- Personal experiences of substantial and chronic social disadvantage in American society, not in other countries.
- Negative impact on entry into or advancement in the business world because of the disadvantage.

SBA will consider education, employment and business history, where applicable, to see if the totality of circumstances shows disadvantage in entering into or advancing in the business world.

- Education: SBA considers such factors as denial of equal access to institutions of higher education, exclusion from social and professional association with students or teachers, denial of educational honors rightfully earned, and social patterns or pressures, which discouraged the individual from pursuing a professional or business education.
- Employment: SBA considers such factors as unequal treatment in hiring, promotions and other aspects of professional advancement, pay and fringe benefits, and other terms and conditions of employment, retaliatory or discriminatory behavior by an employer, and social patterns or pressures which have channeled the individual into non-professional or non-business fields.
- Business history: SBA considers such factors as unequal access to credit or capital, acquisition of credit or capital under commercially unfavorable circumstances, unequal treatment in opportunities for government contracts or other work, unequal

treatment by potential customers and business associates, and exclusion from business or professional organizations.

Who is considered economically disadvantaged:

- Economically disadvantaged individuals are socially disadvantaged individuals whose ability to compete in the free enterprise system has been impaired due to diminished capital and credit opportunities as compared to others in the same or similar line of business that are not socially disadvantaged.
- For initial eligibility the net worth of an individual claiming to be economically disadvantaged must be less than $250,000. After admission in the program, the net worth must be less than $750,000.

The applicant concern must possess reasonable prospects for success in competing in the private sectors if admitted to the 8a Business Development program. To do so, it must be in business in its primary industry classification for at least two full years immediately prior to the date of its 8a Business Development application, unless a waiver for this requirement is granted.

- Income tax returns for each of the two previous tax years must show operating revenues in the primary industry in which the applicant is seeking 8a Business Development certification.

The Small Business Administration may waive the two years in business requirements if each of the following five conditions are met:

- The individual or individuals upon whom eligibility is based have substantial business management experience
- The applicant has demonstrated technical experience to carry out its business plan with a substantial likelihood for success if admitted to the 8a Business Development program

- The applicant has adequate capital to sustain its operations and carry out its business plan as a Participant
- The applicant has a record of successful performance on contracts from governmental or non-governmental sources in its primary industry category
- The applicant has, or can demonstrate his/her ability to obtain in a timely manner, the personnel, facilities, equipment, and any other requirements needed to perform contracts as a Participant

The concern seeking a waiver must provide information on governmental and non-governmental contracts in progress and completed (including letters of reference) in order to establish successful contract performance, and must demonstrate how it otherwise meets the five conditions for waiver. SBA considers an applicant's performance on both government and private sector contracts in determining whether the firm has an overall successful performance record. If, however, the applicant has performed only government contracts or only private sector contracts, SBA will review its performance on those contracts alone to determine whether the applicant possesses a record of successful performance.

- In assessing potential for success, SBA considers the concern's access to credit and capital, including, but not limited to, access to long-term financing, access to working capital financing, equipment trade credit, access to raw materials and supplier trade credit, and bonding capability.

- In assessing potential for success, SBA will also consider the technical and managerial experience of the applicant concern's managers, the operating history of the concern, the concern's record of performance on previous Federal and private sector contracts in the primary industry in which the concern is seeking 8a Business Development certification, and its financial capacity. The applicant concern as a whole must demonstrate both technical knowledge in its primary industry category and management experience sufficient to run its day-to-day operations.

- The Participant or individuals employed by the Participant must hold all requisite licenses if the concern is engaged in an industry requiring professional licensing.

An applicant will not be denied admission into the 8a Business Development program due solely to a determination that potential 8a contract opportunities are unavailable to assist in the development of the concern unless:

- The Government has not previously procured and is unlikely to procure the types of products or services offered by the concern, or
- The purchase of such products or services by the Federal Government will not be in quantities sufficient to support the developmental needs of the applicant and other Participants providing the same or similar items or services.

Other eligibility requirements that apply for individuals or businesses:
- Good character: The applicant or Participant and all its principals must have good character.
- If, during the processing of an application, adverse information is obtained from the applicant or a credible source regarding possible criminal conduct by the applicant or any of its principals, no further action will be taken on the application until SBA's Inspector General has collected relevant information and has advised the AA/8a BD of his or her findings. The AA/8a BD will consider those findings when evaluating the application.
- Violations of any of SBA's regulations may result in denial of participation in the 8a BD program. The AA/8a BD will consider

the nature and severity of the violation in making an eligibility determination.

- Debarred or suspended concerns or concerns owned by debarred or suspended persons are ineligible for admission to the 8a BD program.
- An applicant is ineligible for admission to the 8a BD program if the applicant concern or a proprietor, partner, limited liability member, director, officer, or holder of at least 10 percent of its stock, or another person (including key employees) with significant authority over the concern:
- Lacks business integrity as demonstrated by information related to an indictment or guilty plea, conviction, civil judgment, or settlement; or
- Is currently incarcerated, or on parole or probation pursuant to a pre-trial diversion or following conviction for a felony or any crime involving business integrity.

If, during the processing of an application, SBA determines that an applicant has knowingly submitted false information, regardless of whether correct information would cause SBA to deny the application, and regardless of whether correct information was given to SBA in accompanying documents, SBA will deny the application.

If, after admission to the program, SBA discovers that a firm has knowingly submitted false information, SBA will initiate termination proceedings and suspend the firm.

One-time eligibility: Once a concern or disadvantaged individual upon whom eligibility was based has participated in the 8a BD program, neither the concern nor that individual will be eligible again.

- Use of eligibility will take effect on the date of the concern's approval for admission into the program.
- An individual who uses his or her one-time eligibility to qualify a concern for the 8a BD program will be considered a non-

disadvantaged individual for ownership or control purposes of
another applicant or Participant. The criteria restricting
participation by non-disadvantaged individuals will apply to
such an individual.

- When at least 50% of the assets of a concern are the same as
those of a former Participant, the concern will not be eligible for
entry into the program.
- Participants which change their form of business organization
and transfer their assets and liabilities to the new organization
may do so without affecting the eligibility of the new
organization provided the previous business is dissolved and all
other eligibility criteria are met. In such a case, the new
organization may complete the remaining program term of the
previous organization. A request for a change in business form
will be treated as a change of ownership.
- Wholesalers: An applicant concern seeking admission to the 8a
BD program as a wholesaler need not demonstrate that it is
capable of meeting the requirements of the non-manufacturer
rule for its primary industry classification.
- Brokers: Brokers are ineligible to participate in the 8a BD
program. A broker is a concern that adds no material value to an
item being supplied to a procuring activity or which does not
take ownership or possession of or handle the item being
procured with its own equipment or facilities.
- Federal financial obligations: Neither a firm nor any of its
principals that fails to pay significant financial obligations owed
to the Federal Government, including unresolved tax liens and
defaults on Federal loans or other Federally assisted financing, is
eligible for admission to or participation in the 8a BD program
- Achievement of benchmarks: Where actual participation by
disadvantaged businesses in a particular SIC Major Group
exceeds the benchmark limitations established by the
Department of Commerce, SBA, in its discretion, may decide
not to accept an application for 8a BD participation from a
concern whose primary industry classification falls within that
Major Group.

- Any concern or any individual on behalf of a business has the right to apply for 8a BD program participation whether or not there is an appearance of eligibility.
- An application for 8a BD program admission must be filed in the SBA Division of Program Certification and Eligibility (DPCE) field office serving the territory in which the principal place of business is located. The SBA district office will provide an applicant concern with information regarding the 8a BD program and with all required application forms.
- Each 8a BD applicant concern must submit those forms and attachments required by SBA when applying for admission to the 8a BD program. These forms and attachments will include, but not be limited to, financial statements, Federal personal and business tax returns, and personal history statements. An applicant must also submit IRS Form 4506, Request for Copy or Transcript of Tax Form, to SBA. The application package may be in the form of an electronic application.

Source: http://www.sba.gov/GC/FAQs-mar2005.pdf

http://www.sba.gov/content/8a-business-development/

Native Americans

❧

Small Disadvantaged Business (SDB) Eligibility
- Only small firms that are owned and controlled by socially and economically disadvantaged individuals are eligible to participate in Federal SDB price evaluation adjustment, evaluation factor or sub factor, monetary subcontracting incentive, or set-aside programs, or SBA's section 8(d) subcontracting program.
- In order for a concern to represent that it is an SDB as a prime contractor for purposes of a Federal Government procurement, it must have:
- Received a certification from SBA that it qualifies as an SDB or
- Submitted an application for SDB certification to SBA or a Private Certifier, and must not have received a negative determination regarding that application from SBA or the Private Certifier.
- A firm cannot represent itself to be an SDB concern in order to receive a preference as an SDB for any Federal subcontracting program if it is not on the SBA-maintained list of qualified SDBs.

What is a Small Disadvantaged Business (SDB)?

- Reliance on 8(a) criteria. In determining whether a firm qualifies as an SDB, the criteria of social and economic disadvantage and other eligibility requirements established, including the requirements of ownership and control and disadvantaged status, unless otherwise provided in this subpart. Qualified Private Certifiers must use the 8(a) criteria applicable to ownership and control in determining whether a particular firm is actually owned and controlled by one or more individuals claiming disadvantaged status.

A small disadvantaged business (SDB) is a concern:

- Which qualifies as small under part 121 of this title for the size standard corresponding to the applicable four-digit Standard Industrial Classification (SIC) code.
- For purposes of SDB certification, the applicable SIC code is that which relates to the primary business activity of the concern
- For purposes related to a specific Federal Government contract, the applicable SIC code is assigned by the contracting officer to the procurement at issue
- Which is at least 51% unconditionally owned by one or more socially and economically disadvantaged individuals
- Except for tribes, ANCs, NHOs, and CDCs, whose management and daily business operations are controlled by one or more socially and economically disadvantaged individuals
- Which, for purposes of SDB procurement mechanisms authorized by 10 U.S.C. 2323 (such as price evaluation adjustments, evaluation factors or sub factors, monetary subcontracting incentives, or SDB set-asides) relating to the Department of Defense, NASA and the Coast Guard only, has the majority of its earnings accruing directly to the socially and economically disadvantaged individuals.

Disadvantaged status: In assessing the personal financial condition of an individual claiming economic disadvantage, his or her net worth must be less than $750,000 after taking into account the exclusions

Additional eligibility criteria:

- Except for tribes, ANCs, CDCs and NHOs, each individual claiming disadvantaged status must be a citizen of the United States.
- Potential for success not required.

Joint ventures

Joint ventures are permitted for SDB procurement mechanisms (such as price evaluation adjustments, evaluation factors or sub factors, monetary subcontracting incentives, or SDB set-asides), provided that the requirements set forth in this paragraph are met.

The disadvantaged participant(s) to the joint venture must have:

- Received an SDB certification from SBA; or
- Submitted an application for SDB certification to SBA or a Private Certifier, and must not have received a negative determination regarding that application.
- For purposes of this section, the term joint venture means two or more concerns forming an association to engage in and carry out a single, specific business venture for joint profit. Two or more concerns that form an ongoing relationship to conduct business would not be considered ``joint ventures" within the meaning of this paragraph, and would also not be eligible to be certified as an SDB. The entity created by such a relationship would not be owned and controlled by one or more socially and economically disadvantaged individuals. Each contract for which a joint venture submits an offer will be evaluated on a case-by-case basis.
- A concern that is owned and controlled by one or more socially and economically disadvantaged individuals entering into a joint venture agreement with one or more other business concerns is considered to be affiliated with such other concern(s) for size purposes. If the exception does not apply, the combined annual receipts or employees of the concerns entering into the joint venture must meet the applicable size standard corresponding to the SIC code designated for the contract.
- An SDB must be the managing venture of the joint venture, and an employee of the managing venture must be the project manager responsible for performance of the contract.

- The joint venture must perform any applicable percentage of work required of SDB offers and the SDB joint ventures(s) must perform a significant portion of the contract.

Ownership restrictions for non-disadvantaged individuals:

- The ownership restrictions set forth for non-disadvantaged individuals and concerns do not apply for purposes of determining SDB eligibility.

What is a Private Certifier?

- A Private Certifier is an organization or business concern approved by SBA to determine whether firms are owned and controlled by one or more individuals claiming disadvantaged status. SBA may elect to arrange for one or more Private Certifiers to perform certain functions in the SDB Certification process. SBA will establish more detailed standards regarding qualifications, monitoring, procedures and use, if any, of Private Certifiers in specific contracts or agreements between SBA and the Private Certifiers.

How does an organization or business concern become a Private Certifier?

- SBA may execute contracts or agreements with organizations or business concerns seeking to become Private Certifiers. Any such contract or agreement will include provisions for the oversight, monitoring, and evaluation of all certification activities by SBA.
- The organization or business concern must demonstrate a knowledge of SBA's regulations regarding ownership and control, as well as business organizations and the legal principles affecting their ownership and control generally, including stock issuances, voting rights, convertibility of debt to equity, options,

and powers and responsibilities of officers and directors, general and limited partners, and limited liability members.

- The organization or concern must also, along with its principals, demonstrate good character. Good character does not exist for these purposes if the organization or concern or any of its principals:
  - Is debarred or suspended under any Federal procurement or non-procurement debarment and suspension regulations; or
  - Has been indicted or convicted for any criminal offense or suffered a civil judgment indicating a lack of business integrity.
- As a condition of approval, SBA may require that appropriate officers and/or key employees of the concern attend a training session on SBA's rules and requirements.
- An organization or concern seeking to become a Private Certifier must agree to provide access to SBA of its books and records when requested, including records pertaining to its certification activities. Once SBA approves the organization or concern to be a Private Certifier, SBA may review this information, as well as the decisions of the Private Certifier, in determining whether it will renew or extend the term of the Private Certifier, or terminate the Private Certifier for cause.
- SBA will include in any contract or agreement document authorizing an entity to act as a Private Certifier appropriate conditions to prohibit conflicts of interests between the Private Certifier and the firms for which it processes SDB applications and to protect the integrity of the decision-making process.

Is there a list of Private Certifiers?

- SBA will maintain a list of approved Private Certifiers on SBA's Home Page on the Internet. Any interested person may also obtain a copy of the list from the local SBA district office.

How does a firm become certified as an SDB?

- Any firm may apply to be certified as an SDB. SBA's field offices will provide further information and required application forms to any firm interested in SDB certification. In order to become certified as an SDB, a firm must apply to SBA or, if directed by SBA, to a Private Certifier. The application must include evidence demonstrating that the firm is owned and controlled by one or more individuals claiming disadvantaged status, along with certifications or narratives regarding the disadvantaged status of such individuals. The firm also must submit information necessary for a size determination. Current 8(a) BD Participants do not need to submit applications for SDB status. These concerns automatically qualify as SDBs by virtue of their status as 8(a) BD concerns. An 8(a) Participant's continuing eligibility as an SDB will be reviewed as part of the concern's 8(a) annual review.

Filing an SDB application

- An interested firm must first submit a complete application to SBA's Assistant Administrator for Small Disadvantaged Business Certification and Eligibility (AA/SDBCE), Small Business Administration, 409 3rd Street, SW, Washington, DC 20416, or to a specific SBA field office or an approved Private Certifier if directed by SBA.
- The firm must identify which individual(s) or entities are claiming disadvantaged status.

Required forms

- Each firm seeking to be certified as an SDB must submit those forms and attachments required by SBA when applying for admission to the 8(a) BD program. These forms and attachments may include, but not be limited to: financial statements, Federal personal and business tax returns and personal history statements. The application package may be in the form of an electronic application.

Application processing

- SBA or a Private Certifier will advise each applicant generally within 15 days after the receipt of an application whether the application is complete and suitable for evaluation and, if not, what additional information or clarification is required. If the application is not complete, SBA or the Private Certifier will return the application to the firm, and will notify the firm that it may reapply when its application is complete.
- The burden is on the applicant to demonstrate that those individuals claiming disadvantaged status own and control the concern.

Ownership and control decision

- SBA or a Private Certifier will determine whether those individuals claiming disadvantaged status own and control the applicant firm within 30 days of receipt of a complete application package, whenever practicable.
- Where a Private Certifier determines ownership and control, the Private Certifier will issue a written decision as to whether the applicant is owned and controlled by the individuals identified as claiming disadvantaged status.
- If the Private Certifier finds that the applicant is owned and controlled by the individuals claiming disadvantaged status, the Private Certifier will forward the application to SBA along with a copy of its ownership and control determination and the information required.
- If the Private Certifier finds that the applicant is not owned and controlled by the individuals claiming disadvantaged status, its decision must state the specific reasons for the finding, and inform the applicant of its right to appeal the decision to SBA.

- Where SBA determines ownership and control, SBA will first determine whether the applicant is owned and controlled by the individual(s) claiming to be disadvantaged. If SBA determines that the applicant is not owned and controlled by the individual(s) claiming disadvantaged status, SBA will issue a written decision addressing only the ownership and control issues. If SBA determines that the applicant is owned and controlled by the individual(s) claiming disadvantaged status, SBA will issue a single written decision as to whether the applicant qualifies as an SDB. Such a determination will include the ownership and control of the firm, the size status of the firm, and the disadvantaged status of those individuals claiming to be disadvantaged.
- In its sole discretion, SBA may analyze and determine whether a firm is owned and controlled by one or more individuals claiming disadvantaged status notwithstanding the availability of a Private Certifier to make such a decision.
- SBA reserves the right to re-evaluate an approved decision on ownership and control by a Private Certifier in a case where it has credible evidence that the Private Certifier has substantially disregarded the eligibility criteria.

Disadvantaged determination

- Once a concern receives a decision finding that it is owned and controlled by those individuals or entities claiming disadvantaged status (either through an initial determination or on appeal), SBA will determine whether the other eligibility criteria are met and, if so, will include the SDB on the SBA-maintained list of qualified SDBs. SBA will make this determination within 30 days of receiving an SDB application, if practicable.

Members of designated groups

- Those individuals claiming disadvantaged status that are members of the same designated groups that are presumed to be socially disadvantaged for purposes of SBA's 8(a) BD program are presumed to be socially and economically disadvantaged for purposes of SDB certification. These individuals must represent that they are members of one of the designated groups, that they are identified as a member of one of the designated groups, that their net worth is less than $750,000 after taking into account the exclusions, and that they are citizens of the United States.
- Absent credible evidence to the contrary, SBA may accept these representations as true and certify the firm as an SDB. Individuals not members of designated groups
- Each individual claiming disadvantaged status who is not a member of one of the designated groups must submit a statement identifying personally how his or her entry into or advancement in the business world has been impaired because of personally specific factors and how his or her ability to compete in the free enterprise system has been impaired due to diminished capital and credit opportunities
- Where a Private Certifier determines ownership and control, the Private Certifier must also review the disadvantaged status submission and any other required information, and send to SBA the following:
- An executive summary and analysis of the disadvantaged status submission
- The application and all supporting documentation, and
- A certification that the application is complete and suitable for evaluation.
- Concerns owned by tribes, ANCs, CDCs, or NHOs: SBA will process SDB applications from concerns owned and controlled by tribes, ANCs, CDCs, or NHOs in the same way as those from concerns owned by individuals who are members of designated groups.

SDB Determination

- If SBA's AA/SDBCE determines that the individual(s) claiming disadvantage are disadvantaged and other eligibility criteria are met, he or she will certify the firm as an SDB.

- If SBA's AA/SDBCE determines that one or more of the individuals claiming to be disadvantaged is not disadvantaged and their disadvantaged status is required to establish disadvantaged ownership and control of the applicant, or any of the other eligibility criteria are not met, he or she will reject the firm's application for SDB certification. The AA/SDBCE will issue a written decision setting forth SBA's reasons for decline.

- If the AA/SDBCE declines the firm's application for SDB certification, the firm may request that the AA/SDBCE reconsider his or her initial decline by submitting a written request to the AA/SDBCE within 45 days of the date of the AA/SDBCE's decision. The applicant may provide any additional information and documentation pertinent to overcoming the reason(s) for the initial decline.

- The AA/SDBCE will issue a written decision within 30 days of receiving the applicant's request for reconsideration, if practicable. The AA/SDBCE may approve the application, deny it on one or more of the same grounds as the initial decision, or deny it on other grounds. If the application is denied, the AA/SDBCE will explain why the applicant is not eligible for SDB certification and give specific reasons for the decline. If the AA/SDBCE declines the application solely on issues not raised in the initial decline, the applicant may request another reconsideration as if it were an initial decline. If the AA/SDBCE declines the application for one or more of the same reasons as addressed in the initial decline, the applicant is not entitled to a second reconsideration.

- A firm may appeal to OHA the AA/SDBCE's decision that one or more of the individuals claiming disadvantaged status is not disadvantaged, or, where SBA determines

THE GOVERNMENT CONTRACTOR'S RESOURCE GUIDE

ownership and control, that those claiming disadvantaged status do not own and control the applicant.

- The firm must serve SBA's Associate General Counsel for Procurement Law with a copy of the appeal.
- OHA will determine whether SBA's decision in either case was arbitrary, capricious, or contrary to law. OHA's review is limited to the facts that were before SBA at the time of its decision and any arguments submitted in or in response to the appeal. OHA will not consider any facts beyond those that were already presented to SBA unless the administrative judge determines that manifest injustice would occur if the appeal were limited to the record.
- A firm may also request a formal size determination pursuant to where SBA finds that the firm is not small.
- Current 8(a) BD program participants.
- Any firm that is currently a Participant in SBA's 8(a) BD program need not seek an ownership and control determination or apply to SBA for a separate certification as an SDB. SBA will certify current 8(a) BD Participants as SDBs, and automatically include them on the list of qualified SDBs.
- 8(a) BD graduates
- SBA will automatically certify a firm that has graduated from the SBA's 8(a) BD program to be an SDB, provided SBA determined that the firm continued to be eligible for the 8(a) BD program as part of an annual review within the last three years.
- Certification by DOT recipient
- If a firm applying for SDB certification has a current, valid certification as a disadvantaged business enterprise (DBE) from a Department of Transportation (DOT) recipient, SBA may adopt the DBE certification as an SDB certification when determined by the AA/SDBCE or designee to be appropriate.

Service Disabled Veterans Assistant

❊

Veteran and service-connected disability means:

- The term "veteran" means a person who served in the active military, naval, or air service, and who was discharged or released under conditions other than dishonorable. The term "service connected" means, with respect to disability or death, that such disability was incurred or aggravated, or that the death resulted from a disability incurred or aggravated, in line of duty in the active military, naval, or air service. An injury or disease incurred during military service will be deemed to have been incurred in the line of duty unless the disability was caused by the veteran's own misconduct or abuse of alcohol or drugs, or was incurred while absent without permission or while confined by military or civilian authorities for serious crimes.

How does a veteran verify their status as a service disabled veteran?

To be considered a Service-Disabled Veteran, the veteran must have an adjudication letter from the Veterans Administration (VA), a Department of Defense Form 214, Certificate of Release or Discharge from Active Duty, or a Statement of Service from the National Archives and Records Administration, stating that the veteran has a service-connected disability.

What is a service-disabled, veteran-owned, small business concern?

A small business concern owned and controlled by a Service-Disabled Veteran or Service Disabled Veterans, as defined in section 3 of the Small Business Act and SBA's implementing SDVO SBC Program Regulations.

Is there a formal certification process required from the SBA to participate in the SDVOSB procurement program?

No. The Veterans Benefits Act of 2003 that established restricted contracting in Federal procurement for Service-Disabled Veteran-Owned Small Business Concerns (SDVO SBC) did not require a formal process to certify concerns as SDVO SBC. A SDVO SBC self-represents its status for all Federal contracts. In order to place an offer on a Federal contract, the SBC must be registered in the Government's Central Contractor Registration (CCR). Once the SBC is registered in CCR, and an offer is submitted on a Federal Contract, the SDVO SBC will need to fill out an "On-Line Representations and Certifications Application."

What eligibility requirements must a small business concern meet to participate in the SDVO SBC procurement program?

The concern must be a small business pursuant to the North American Industrial Classification System (NAICS) code assigned by the Contracting Officer to the procurement, the concern must be 51% unconditionally and directly owned by one or more Service-Disabled Veterans or in the case of any publicly owned business, not less than 51% of the stock of the company is owned by one or more Service-Disabled Veterans, and the management and daily business operations of the SDVO SBC must be controlled by one or more service-disabled veterans (or in the case of a veteran with permanent and severe disability, the spouse or permanent caregiver of such veteran).

3   77 - 79   Events To Attend

Events to Attend

❖

Business Match Making

Business Match making, a partnership between the U.S. Small Business Administration, SCORE and HP, offers many opportunities for small businesses to participate in the procurement opportunities offered by government agencies and major corporations. The program unites education, training, counseling, key resources and tools with actual face-to-face and "virtual" match making meeting opportunities with procurement representatives from the public and private sector. Based on the generosity of HP and additional private sector co-sponsors, Business Matchmaking continues to be a program offered at no cost to its participants. For matchmaking events near you visit:
http://www.businessmatchmaking. com/.

Department of Defense (DoD) Official Mail Management Workshop

Sponsored by the Military Postal Service Agency, the DoD Official Mail Manager Workshop offers training for all Department of Defense agencies and is open to all federal agencies. Training includes basic technical postal information such as: how to reduce postage costs, computing postage, classes of mail, special services, postage meter management, U.S. Postal Service automation, and the Private Express Statutes.

Federal Mail Symposium:

Sponsored by GSA, the First Federal Mail Symposium is open to all federal agencies. The workshops will address issues that relate to federal mail employees and discuss new trends in federal mail management, technology, security, safety, policies, and other federal mail center operations issues.

Government Mailers Advisory Council (GMAC) Meetings
GMAC is an active partnership of members from the federal mailing community and the U.S. Postal Service in Washington, DC. Formed in August 1994, GMAC is a forum for sharing ideas, suggestions and solutions to improve mail services. The GMAC has made major strides in standardized addressing and reducing misdirected mail. GMAC's membership includes federal mail managers in the Washington DC area that are served by Washington DC post offices.

GSA Expo
The GSA Expo is a free training conference and trade show exposition designed for all levels of government personnel who make or influence, procurement decisions. You can access information about any upcoming GSA expos by visiting: http://www.expo.gsa.gov/.

Interagency Mail Policy Council (IMPC) Quarterly Meetings
The Interagency Mail Policy Council (IMPC) is a group of federal employees that meets on a quarterly basis to share mail management information, best practices, and provide training. The IMPC was established in 1997 and is officially chartered by the Administrator of the GSA.

Local Events
To find local events to attend in your area you can access the following web site: http://www.sba.gov/calendar/. This link will take you to a map of the United States. To access this site, click on the state your business resides in, and the link will take you to a page of upcoming events in your area.

For more Government Business Matchmaking events to attend in your area, please contact your regional SBA office. A comprehensive list of regional offices is provided in Chapter 5.

4   81 - 88   Web Sites to Visit

Websites to Visit

❧

http://www.acq.osd.mil/

AcqWeb is the official web site of the Office of the Under Secretary of Defense for Acquisition, Technology, and Logistics. It is a publicly-accessible site and contains vast amounts of information about our functions, activities, and projects. Our mission is to advise the Secretary of Defense on all matters pertaining to the Department of Defense's acquisition process, research and development; advanced technology; test and evaluation; production; logistics; military construction; procurement; economic security; and atomic energy.

http://www.afei.org/

The Association For Enterprise Integration will help you to build government and industry inter-relationships and to help you to promote the development of a global information infrastructure.

http://www.ccr.gov/

The Central Contractor Registration Web site is the first place companies must start at in order to receive government contracts.

http://www.coalgovpro.org/

The Coalition for Government Procurement (CGP) is a non-profit association of companies that sell commercial services and products to the federal government primarily through multiple award schedule (MAS) contracts and GWACs. The Coalition's mission is to protect the interest of its members by providing valuable information on issues affecting the government market and by constantly advocating common sense in government procurement policy.

http://www.dnb.com/

The Dun & Bradstreet Web site is where companies must go in order to receive their D-U-N-S Number to finish registering at The Central Contractor Registration Web site.

http://www.ebuy.gsa.gov/

GSA's latest e-Business innovation, e-Buy, is an electronic Request for Quote (RFQ) / Request for Proposal (RFP) system designed to allow Federal buyers to request information, find sources, and prepare RFQs/RFPs, online, for millions of services and products offered through GSA's Multiple Award Schedule (MAS) and Government wide Acquisition Contracts(GWAC).

http://www.expo.gsa.gov/

FREE Training Conference and Trade Show Exposition designed for all levels of government personnel who make or influence, procurement decisions.

http://www.export.gov/

Export.gov shows businesses upcoming trade show events and gives useful information on how to export their business to other countries.

http://www.fedbizopps.gov/

FedBizOpps.gov is the single government point-of-entry (GPE) for Federal government procurement opportunities over $25,000. Government buyers are able to publicize their business opportunities by posting information directly to FedBizOpps via the Internet. Through one portal - FedBizOpps (FBO) – commercial vendors seeking Federal markets for their products and services can search, monitor and retrieve opportunities solicited by the entire Federal contracting community.

http://www.fedworld.gov/

The FedWorld.gov web site is a gateway to government information. This site is managed by the National Technical Information Service (NTIS) as part of its information management mandate.

http://www.firstgov.gov/

Whatever you want or need from the U.S. government, it's here on FirstGov.gov. You'll find a rich treasure of online information, services and resources.

https://www.fpds.gov/

Federal Procurement Data System: find out what's new, place a request, download a report, and find many important links when you register on our Web site.

http://www.geia.org/

GEIA represents the high technology industry that provides proven solutions to meet the needs of the Government customer. Our members develop, integrate and deploy electronic and information technology (IT) products and services to meet exacting Federal requirements. In partnership with our member companies and their government customers, GEIA studies the market for IT, research & technology, and advanced electronics products and services for defense and civil government agencies. We then produce annually a 10-Year Defense Forecast, a 5-year Federal IT Forecast, and special studies on key markets such as Homeland Security, Services & Support, Information Assurance, etc.

http://www.gpo.gov/davisbacon/

The Davis Bacon Wage Determinations site allows users to see the wage determinations issued by the U.S. Department of Labor to be paid on federally funded or assisted construction projects.

http://www.gsa.gov/

The General Services Administration provides employment opportunities, acquisition solutions, e-Tools, events, references, news releases, training programs, and organizational methods to help other agencies better serve the public by meeting – at best value – their needs for products and services, and to simplify citizen access to government information and services.

http://www.gsa.gov/sbu/
GSA's Office of Small Business Utilization (OSBU) advocates for small, minority, veteran, HUBZone, and women business owners. Its mission is to promote increased access to GSA's nationwide procurement opportunities.

http://www.house.gov/
US House of Representatives

http://www.nao.usace.army.mil/
The U.S. Army Corps of Engineers shows labor standards for Government contracts, as well as how to do register for their solicitations and different federal business opportunities they have available.

http://www.nnmsa.org/
The Northern New Mexico Supplier Alliance (NNMSA) is a member-driven organization that exists to promote small business growth and economic development through job creation and business creation/expansion in Northern New Mexico. All NNMSA sponsored activities and strategic initiatives are directed at helping our members be ready for tomorrow's business opportunities today. NNMSA is here to help its members meet everyday business challenges, manage the risks associated with doing business, and identify new opportunities for ongoing business growth and development.

http://www.opm.gov/
The Office of Personnel Management serves as the authoritative source for statistical information on the size and composition of the federal civilian workforce. OPM offers customers free electronic

publications that contain hundreds of tables and charts and specialized services for customers who need additional data or statistics.

http://www.osdbu.gov/

The Federal OSDBU Directors Interagency Council site allows users to go to different Federal OSDBU offices, as well as information about OSDBU.

http://www.pueblo.gsa.gov/

This is a consolidated site that provides electronic access to various federal entities.

http://www.sba.gov/gulf/gulfstates_bmm.html/

Business Matchmaking, a partnership between the U.S. Small Business Administration, SCORE and HP, continues in 2006 with even greater opportunities for small businesses to participate in the procurement opportunities offered by government agencies and major corporations. The program unites education, training, counseling, key resources, and tools with actual face-to-face and "virtual" matchmaking meeting opportunities with procurement representatives from the public and private sector. Based on the generosity of HP and additional private sector co-sponsors, Business Matchmaking continues to be a program offered at no costs to its participants.

http://www.sba.gov/businessop/index.html

The Small Business Administration Business Opportunities shows one the basics on selling goods and services to the government, from understanding the rules to knowing how to write a contract proposal.

http://www.sbanetwork.org/

Gives tips on how to effectively start and manage your own business.

http://www.senate.gov/
US Senate

http://www.the-dma.org/
The Direct Marketing Association is the leading global trade association of business and nonprofit organizations using and supporting direct marketing tools and techniques.

http://www.trade.gov/mas/
The U.S. Department of Commerce International Trade Administration offers an easy access to services to help small businesses increase their export potential.

http://www.whitehouse.gov/government/cabinet/
Displays the current Cabinet of the President of the United States

http://www.whitehouse.gov/government/independentagencies.html/
This site is an alphabetical index with links to various federal agencies and commissions.

http://www.whitehouse.gov/government/judg.html/
Judicial Branch Links

http://www.whitehouse.gov/government/eop.html/
White House Offices & Agencies

http://www.sbaonline.sba.gov/financing/special/women.html
Women business owners are critically important to the American economy. America's 9.1 million women-owned businesses employ 27.5 million people and contribute $3.6 trillion to the economy. However, women continue to face unique obstacles in the world of business. The SBA is a very strong advocate for women entrepreneurs and offers many programs and services to help them succeed. The following resources offer unique opportunities and guidance for women entrepreneurs.

http://www.arnet.gov/far/

It is imperative to familiarize yourself with Federal Acquisition Regulations (FAR). Of particular importance to Government Contracting is FAR Part 19 (Small Business Programs). This Web site offers the entire Federal Acquisition Regulation book in a downloadable PDF format.

5   89 -110   Contact listings of OSDBUs and SBA Offices

Small Businesses can expect that the OSDBU will:

❋

- Make the depth and breadth of the services that can be expected from the OSDBU very clear up front,
- Be exceptionally candid as to whether the capabilities of the small business match the agency's needs, and, if not, direct them to the appropriate OSDBU or prime contractor Small Business Liaison Officer (SBLO), preferably with a personal introduction,
- Explain the relevant laws enacted for their benefit, i.e., small business set-asides, 8(a) set-asides, HUBZone set-asides, subcontracting goals, and illustrate how the small business can use them to maximize contract and subcontract opportunities,
- Put them in contact with the appropriate project/technical managers, end users, or any other relevant personnel, assuming the small business is selling what the OSDBU's agency is buying,
- Inform small businesses with all up-to-date information in light of the ever-changing procurement legislation and implementing regulations that impact small business,
- Be a "marketing consultant," "information broker," and facilitator to the small business, e.g., inform it of any special unwritten and cultural nuances or procedures at the OSDBU's agency and its buying activities which will improve the small business' chances of winning a contract,
- Make very clear that certification as an 8(a), small disadvantaged business, HUBZone contractor, service disabled veteran does not create an entitlement to a contract or a guarantee for one in the future, • Stress that understanding the agency's procurement process, engaging in strong marketing, and competing for work, even sole source work, is critical to enhancing one's prospects of obtaining a contract,
- Ensure a professionally-conducted meeting with time parameters and expectations set in advance,

- Summarize the agency's contracting opportunities at its various contracting activities and field installations for the small business' specific area of business or make referrals to those places where the small business can go to obtain such knowledge,
- Demonstrate, if necessary, how to navigate within the agency's host website and highlight the most useful sites and links,
- Offer follow-up due date for responding to questions for which the OSDBU counselor does not have an immediate answer,
- Impart knowledge about the "market" (what the OSDBU's agency buys), the decision makers (agency key players) and the competitive environment at the agency (who the incumbents are, what service needs are growing, which are declining, where the future strategic, long-term opportunities are, etc.),
- Not give false hope, vague or generic information, such as stating how many millions or billions of dollars the agency spends on goods and services with no explanation as to how the small business can reasonably expect to fit into the agency's procurement structure or system,
- Treat all small businesses the same under like circumstances when providing pertinent procurement information and not show special preference to a network of friends or acquaintances, and
- Provide information on the agency's latest acquisition-related initiatives and agency-unique programs that will, or were designed to, increase the chances of a small business to obtain a contract or subcontract, e.g. discuss agency's mentor protégé program, if applicable.
- The Offices of Small and Disadvantaged Business Utilization (OSDBUs) offer small business information on procurement opportunities, guidance on procurement procedures, and identification of both prime and subcontracting opportunities.

Defense Contract Management Agency (DCMA)

Website:	http://www.dcma.mil/DCMAHQ/dcma-sb/index.htm
Address:	Set up by Divisions (Contact office to obtain address)
Phone number:	Toll Free: (877) 662-3960
Director:	Mr. Mark G. Olson (224) 625-8920 mark.olson@dcma.mil
Deputy Director:	Ms. Mary A. Seabolt (804) 734-0418 mary.seabolt@dcma.mil
Comprehensive Subcontracting Rep:	Ms. Margarette Trimble-Williams Comprehensive Subcontracting Division Chief (310) 900-6025
Mentor-Protégé Rep:	Ms. Elaine Howell Division Chief (675) 503-6369
Individual Subcontracting Rep:	Mr. Thomas Watkins East Division Chief (937) 656-3104
Individual Subcontracting Rep:	Ms. DeWillican Middleton West Division Chief (317) 510-2015

Defense Information Systems Agency (DISA)

Website:	http://www.disa.mil
Address:	6916 Cooper Ave., Room 02E32 Ft. Meade Maryland 20755-7901
Director:	Ms. Sharon Jones (301) 225-6004 disasmallbusinessoffice@disa.mil
Deputy Director:	Mr. Anthony Jackson (301) 225-6006

Defense Logistics Agency (DLA)

Website:	http://www.dla.mil/db/
Address:	8725 John J. Kingman Road
	DB Room 1127
	Fort Belvoir, VA 22060-6221
Phone number:	Primary: (703) 767- 0192, Alt: (703) 767-1660
Fax number:	(703) 767-1670
Acting:	Ms. Amy Sajda
	(703) 767-1662
	amy.sajda@dla.mil
8(a)/SDB Rep:	Ms. Patricia Cleveland
	(703) 767-1652
	patricia.cleveland@dla.mil
WOSB Rep:	Ms. Patricia Cleveland
	(703) 767-1652
	patricia.cleveland@dla.mil
HUBZone Rep:	Ms. Peggy Glasheen
	(703) 767-1657
	peggy.glasheen@dla.mil
VO/SDVOSB Rep:	Ms. Peggy Glasheen
	(703) 767-1657
	peggy.glasheen@dla.mil
Subcontracting Rep:	Ms. Peggy Glasheen
	(703) 767-1657
	peggy.glasheen@dla.mil
Mentor-Protégé Rep:	Ms. Peggy Glasheen
	(703) 767-1657
	peggy.glasheen@dla.mil
HBCU/MI Rep:	Ms. Peggy Glasheen
	(703) 767-1657
	peggy.glasheen@dla.mil

Department of the Air Force

Website:	http://www.airforcesmallbiz.org/
Address:	1060 Air Force Pentagon, Room 4268
	Washington DC 20330
Phone number:	(571) 256-8052
Fax number:	(703) 696-1170
Director:	Mr. Joseph McDade
	(571) 256-8052
	joseph.mcdade@pentagon.af.mil
Deputy Director:	Mr. John Caporal
	(571) 256-7761
	john.caporal@pentagon.af.mil
8(a)/SDB Rep:	Ms. Teresa Rendon
	(210) 652-3202
	teresa.rendon@us.af.mil
WOSB Rep:	Ms. Teresa Rendon
	(210) 652-3202
	teresa.rendon@us.af.mil
HUBZone Rep:	Ms. Teresa Rendon
	(210) 652-3202
	teresa.rendon@us.af.mil
VO/SDVOSB Rep:	Mr. Eugene J. Toni
	(571) 256-7762
	eugene.toni@pentagon.af.mil
Subcontracting Rep:	Mr. Tony Peasant
	(571) 256-7765
	tony.peasant@pentagon.af.mil
Mentor-Protégé Rep:	Ms. Grace Fontana
	(571) 256-7757
	grace.fontana@pentagon.af.mill
HBCU/MI Rep:	Ms. Teresa Rendon
	(210) 652-3202
	teresa.rendon@us.af.mil
Other:	Native American/ Tribally Owned Small
	Business
	Ms. Teresa Rendon
	(210) 652-3202
	teresa.rendon@us.af.mil

Department of the Army

Website:	http://www.sellingtoarmy.info/
Address:	The Pentagon, Room 3B514
	Washington, DC 20310-0106
Phone number:	(703) 697-2868
Fax number:	(703) 693-3898
Director:	Ms. Tracey L. Pinson
Deputy Director:	Ms. Suellen Jeffress

Department of Defense

Website:	http://www.acq.osd.mil/osbp/
Address:	4800 Mark Center Drive
	Suite 15G13- East Towers
	Alexandria, VA 22350
Phone number:	(571) 372-6191
Fax number:	(571) 372-6195
Director:	Mr. Andre J. Gudger

Department of Defense Education Activity (DoDEA)

Website:	http://www.dodea.edu/offices/procurement/index.cfm
Address:	4040 N. Fairfax Drive
	Arlington, VA 22203-1635
Phone number:	(703) 588-3625
Fax number:	(703) 588-3704
Director, Small Business	Stephanie Waldrop
Programs:	(703) 588-3625
	smallbusinesspresentative@hq.dodea.edu

Department of the Navy

Website:	http://www.donhq.navy.mil/OSBP
Address:	720 Kennon Street, SE
	Building 36, Room 207
	Washington, DC 20374-5015
Phone number:	(202) 685-6485
Fax number:	(202) 685-6865
Director:	Mr. Sean Crean
	(202) 685-6485
	Sean.Crean@navy.mil
8(a)/SDB Rep:	Mr. Derrick Capers

	(202) 685-6485
	derrick.capers@navy.mil
WOSB Rep:	Ms. Shawn Smith
	(202) 685-6485
	shaw.smith@navy.mil
HUBZone Rep:	Ms. Carlton Hagans
	(202) 685-6485
	carlton.hagans@navy.mil
VO/SDVOSB Rep:	Ms. Carlton Hagans
	(202) 685-6485
	carlton.hagans@navy.mil
Subcontracting Rep:	Ms. Patricia Obey
	(202) 685-6485
	patricia.obey@navy.mil
Mentor-Protégé Rep:	Ms. Oreta Stinson
	(202) 685-6485
	oreta.stinson@navy.mil
Other:	Ms. Shawn Smith
	Program Analyst
	Technical Support
	(202) 685-6485
	shawn.smith4@navy.mil
Other:	Mr. Derrick Capers
	Administrative Assistant
	(202) 685-6485
	derrick.capers@navy.mil

Federal Deposit Insurance Corporation

Website:	http://www.fdic.gov/buying/goods/index.html
Address:	Virginia Square, L. William Seidman Center
	3501 Fairfax Drive, Room E2014
	Arlington, VA 22226
Phone number:	(703) 562-6070
Fax number:	(703) 562-6069
Director:	Mr. Robert Elcan
	Section Chief
	Minority Outreach Program
WOSB Rep:	Ms. Velda Fludd
	Minority Woman Outreach Spec

(703) 562-6071

General Services Administration

Website:	http://www.gsa.gov/smallbusiness
Address:	1275 First Street, NE
	Washington, DC 20417
Phone number:	(202) 208-5938
Fax number:	(202) 501-2590
Associate Administrator:	Ms. Jiyoung C. Park
Deputy Associate Administrator:	Mr. Thomas V. Green Jr.

National Aeronautics and Space Administration

Website:	http://www.osbp.nasa.gov/
Address:	NASA Office of Small Business Programs
	300 E Street, SW
	Washington, DC 20546-0001
Phone number:	(202) 358-2088
Fax number:	(202) 358-3261
Director:	Mr. Glenn A. Delgado
	Associate Administrator
	(202) 358-2088
	smallbusiness@nasa.gov
Policy Rep:	Mr. David B. Grove
	Program Manager
	(202) 358-2088
	smallbusiness@nasa.gov
VOSB, SDVOSB Rep:	Mr. Richard L. Mann
	Program Manager
	(202) 358-2088
	smallbusiness@nasa.gov
Mentor-Protégé, WOSB, SDB, 8(a), HUBZone, HBCU/MI Rep:	Ms. Tabisa T. Tepfer
	Program Manager
	(202) 358-2088
	smallbusiness@nasa.gov

National Science Foundation

Website:	http://www.nsf.gov/
Address:	4201 Wilson Boulevard, Room 527
	Arlington, VA, 22230
Phone number:	(703) 292-7082

Fax number: (703) 292-9055
Director: Mr. Donald Senich

Nuclear Regulatory Commission
Website: http://www.nrc.gov/about-
                                     nrc/overview.html
Address: Office of Small Business and Civil Rights
                                     11555 Rockville Pike, MS 03H08
                                     Rockville, MD 20852
Phone number: (301) 415-7380
Fax number: (301) 415-5953
Director: Ms. Corenthis B. Kelley
SB Program Manager: Ms. Diana Strong
Senior Program Analyst: Mr. Anthony D. Briggs
Office of Management and Budget
(Executive Office of the President)
Website: http://www.whitehouse.gov/omb/
Address: 725 17th Street, NW, Room 5001
                                     Washington, DC 20503
Phone number: (202) 395-7669
Fax number: (202) 395-3982
Director: Ms. Althea A. Kireilis
Small Business Program   Ms. Brenda Spriggs
Administrator: (202)- 395-7669
                                     bspriggs@oa.eop.gov

Smithsonian Institution
Website: http://www.si.edu/oeema/sdbu.htm
Address: Office of Equal Employment and Minority
                                     Affairs
                                     Supplier Diversity Program
                                     P.O. Box 37012, MRC 521
                                     600 Maryland Avenue SW, Suite 2091
                                     Washington, DC 20013-7012
Phone number: (202) 633-6430
Fax number: (202) 633-6427
Director: Ms. Era L. Marshall
SD Program Manager: Mr. Rudy D. Watley
                                     sdphelp@si.edu

Social Security Administration

Website:	http://www.socialsecurity.gov/oag/osdbu/osdbu.htm
Address:	7111 Security Blvd
	1st Floor, Rear Entrance
	Baltimore, MD 21244
Phone number:	(410) 965-7467
Fax number:	(410) 965-2965
Director:	Mr. Wayne McDonald
	wayne.mcdonald@ssa.gov
SADBU Specialist:	Ms. Patricia Bullock
	(410) 965-9457
	pat.bullock@ssa.gov

U.S. Agency for International Development

Website:	http://www.usaid.gov/business/small_business/
Address:	Ronald Reagan Building,
	USAID/OSDBU/MRC
	1300 Pennsylvania Ave., NW
	Room 5.8C
	Washington, DC 20523-5800
Phone number:	(202) 712-1500
Fax number:	(202) 216-3056
Director:	Mr. Mauricio Vera
Deputy Director:	Ms. Kimberly Ball
Senior Small Business Specialist:	Mr. David A. Canada
Senior Program Specialist-Team Leader:	Ms. Teneshia Alston
Small Business Specialist/WOSB:	Ms. Daisy Matthews
Small Business Specialist:	Mr. Kevin Davis
Small Business Specialist:	Ms. Tracy Hembry
Small Business Specialist:	Ms. Sharon Jones Taylor

U.S. Department of Agriculture

Website:	http://www.da.usda.gov/osdbu/
Address:	1400 Independence Avenue, SW.
	Room 1085 - South Building, STOP 9501

	Washington, DC 20250-9501
Phone number:	(202) 720-7117
Fax number:	(202) 720-3001
Acting Director:	Mr. Dexter L. Pearson
	Dexter.pearson@osec.usda.gov
Deputy Director:	Mr. Joe Ware
	Joe.Ware@dm.usda.gov
Associate Director:	Ms. Belinda Ward
	Belinda.Ward@dm.usda.gov
WOSB/Subcontracting Rep:	Ms. Sherry Cohen
	SherryR.Cohen@dm.usda.gov
VO/SDVOSB Rep:	Ms. Linda Epstein
	Linda.Epstein@dm.usda.gov
Procurement Forecast:	Mr. Michael Spencer
	Michael.Spencer@dm.usda.gov
Vendor Outreach Program:	Ms. Janet Baylor
	Janet.Baylor@dm.usda.gov
Program Analyst:	Ms. Michelle Warren
	Michelle.Warren@dm.usda.gov
Program Analyst:	Ms. Roxanne Lane
	Roxanne.Lane@dm.usda.gov

U.S. Department of Commerce

Website:	http://www.osec.doc.gov/osdbu/
Address:	14th & Constitution Avenue, NW
	Room H-6411
	Washington, DC 20230
Phone number:	(202) 482-1472
Fax number:	(202) 482-0501
Director:	Ms. La Juene Desmukes

U.S. Department of Education

Website:	http://www.ed.gov/about/offices/list/ods/osdbu.html
Address:	Potomac Center Plaza, Room 7050
	550 12th St. SW
	Washington, DC 20202
Phone number:	(202) 245-6300
Fax number:	(202) 245-6304

E-mail:	small.business@ed.gov
Director:	Dr. Kristi Wilson Hill
	(202) 245-6300
	Kristi.Wilson@ed.gov
8(a)/SDB Rep:	Ms. Marcella Coverson
	(202) 245-6300
	Marcella.Coverson@ed.gov
WOSB Rep:	Ms. Melanie Carter
	(202) 245-6300
	Melanie.Carter@ed.gov
HUBZone Rep:	Ms. Marcella Coverson
	(202) 245-6300
	Marcella.Coverson@ed.gov
VO/SDVOSB Rep:	Mr. Jerome Newton
	(202) 245-6300
	Jerome.Newton@ed.gov

U.S. Department of Energy

Website:	http://smallbusiness.doe.gov/
Address:	1000 Independence Avenue, S.W.
	Room # 5B-148
	Washington, DC 20585
Phone number:	(202) 586-7377
Fax number:	(202) 586-5488
Director:	Mr. William Valdez
	(202) 586-8383
	William.valdez@hq.doe.gov
Supervisory Acquisition Manager:	Ms. Brenda DeGraffenreid
	(202) 586-4620
	Brenda.DeGrafffenreid@hq.doe.gov
Procurement Analyst:	Mr. Nick Demer
	(202) 586-1614
	Nick.Demer@hq.doe.gov
Small Business Specialist:	Mr. Kent Hibben
	(202) 586-8086
	Kent.Hibben@hq.doe.gov
Small Business Specialist:	Ms. Anita Bedrosian
	(202) 586-2907
	Anita.Bedrosian@hq.doe.gov

Administrative Support Specialist:	Ms. Claudette Williams (202) 586-7377 Claudette.Williams@hq.doe.gov

U.S. Department of Health and Human Services

Website:	http://www.hhs.gov/smallbusiness/
Address:	200 Independence Avenue, S.W. Room 537H Hubert H. Humphrey Building Washington, DC 20201
Phone number:	(202) 690-7300
Fax number:	(202) 205-9882
Director:	Ms. Teresa L.G. Lewis (202) 690-7300 sbmail@hhs.gov
Senior Advisor:	Mr. Clarence Randall (202) 690-8544 Clarence.Randall@HHS.Gov
Subcontracting and Electronic Subcontracting Reporting System (eSRS) Point of Contact:	Ms. Courtney Carter Small Business Specialist (202) 260-6353 Courtney.Carter@hhs.gov
Mentor-Protégé Point of Contact:	Ms. Anita Allen Small Business Specialist (301) 443-1715 Anita.Allen@PSC.hhs.gov
Acquisition Data Calendar of Events:	Ms. Linda M. Purnell Program Analyst (202) 690-7302 linda.purnell@hhs.gov
Outreach Activities and HHS Vendor Outreach Session (VOS) Point of Contact:	Ms. Ruth E. Lewis Program Support Analyst (202) 690-7301 ruth.lewis@hhs.gov

HHS Small Business Specialists

HHS-Agency for Healthcare Research and Quality (AHRQ):	Ms. Debra Stidham (410) 786-5230 Debra.Stidham@cms.hhs.gov
HHS-Centers for Disease	Ms. Allyson Brown

Control and Prevention (CDC):	arbrown@cdc.gov
	Ms. Gwendolyn Miles Gwendolyn.Miles@cdc.hhs.gov
	Main Telephone: (770) 488-3028
HHS-Centers for Medicare and Medicaid Services (CMS):	Ms. Alice P. Roache alice.roache@cms.hhs.gov
	Ms. Debra Stidham Debra.Stidham@cms.hhs.gov
	Main Telephone: (410) 786-5230
HHS-Food and Drug Administration (FDA):	Mr. Wayne Berry (301) 827-1994 Wayne.Berry@fda.hhs.gov
HHS-Health Resources and Services Administration (HRSA):	Ms. Michele McDermott (301) 496-9639 mmcdermott@hrsa.gov
HHS-Indian Health Services (IHS):	Ms. Jonathan Ferguson (301) 496-9639 Jonathan.Ferguson@ihs.hhs.gov
HHS-National Institutes of Health (NIH):	Ms. Annette Owens-Scarboro scarbora@od.nih.gov
	Ms. Nydia Sagna Nydia.Sagna@nih.hhs.gov
	Ms. Michele McDermott mmcdermott@hrsa.gov
	Ms. Jonathan Ferguson Jonathan.Ferguson@ihs.hhs.gov
	Main Telephone: (301) 496-9639
HHS-Program Support Center (PSC):	Ms. Anita Allen (301) 443-1715 Anita.Allen@PSC.hhs.gov
HHS- Substance Abuse and Mental Health Services	Ms. Debra Stidham (410) 786-5230

Administration (SAMSHA):   Debra.Stidham@cms.hhs.gov

U.S. Department of Homeland Security

Website:	http://www.dhs.gov/openforbusiness
Address:	Mailing Address:
	Department of Homeland Security
	245 Murray Ln. SW, Bldg. 410 Room 3124A
	Washington, DC 20528
	Physical Address:
	7th & D Street SW
	Washington, DC 20004
Phone number:	(202) 447-5555
Fax number:	(202) 447-5552
Director:	Mr. Kevin Boshears
Administrative Assistant:	Ms. Candice Brooks
	candice.brooks@dhs.gov
Procurement Analyst:	Ms. Teneshia Alston
	(202) 447-5280
	teneshia.alston@dhs.gov
VO/SDVOSB HUBZone	Mr. Anthony Bell
Representative:	(202) 447-0063
	anthony.bell@dhs.gov
8(a) and SDB Program	Ms. Darlene Bullock
Representative:	(202) 447-5280
	darlene.bullock@dhs.gov
Mentor Protégé Program	Ms. Sharon Davis
Manager:	(202) 447-0104
	sharon.davis@dhs.gov
Subcontracting Program	Mr. Kyle Groome
Representative:	(202) 447-5281
	kyle.groome@dhs.gov
SBA Liaison	Ms. Wendy Hill
Chief of Staff	(202) 447-5286
VOS Coordinator:	wendy.hill@dhs.gov
FPDS-NG and FAR Council	Ms. Sharon Phillips
Representative:	(202) 447-5287
	sharon.phillips@dhs.gov

VOSB/SDVOSB Vendor Outreach Representative:	Mr. Dan Sturdivant (202) 447-5289 dan.sturdivant@dhs.gov
WOSB Program Representative Events Calendar Manager:	Ms. Ilene Waggoner (202) 447-5282 ilene.waggoner@dhs.gov

U.S. Department of Housing and Urban Development

Website:	http://www.hud.gov/offices/osdbu/index.cfm
Address:	451 Seventh Street Room 2200 (SS) Washington, DC 20410-1000
Phone number:	(202) 402-5477
Fax number:	(202) 401-6930
Director:	Ms. Sharman Lancefield Sharman.R.Lancefield@hud.gov
Confidential Assistant:	Ms. Tamika Henson-Giles Tamika.Henson-Giles@hud.gov
Senior Business Utilization Development Specialist:	Ms. Arnette S. McGill-Moore Arnette.S.McGill@hud.gov
Business Utilization Development Specialist:	Ms. Meishoma Hayes Meishoma.A.Hayes@hud.gov
Business Utilization Development Specialist:	Mr. Derek Pruitt Derek.L.Pruitt@hud.gov
Information Receptionist (Intern):	Mr. Elliott Dubose Elliott.R.Dubose@hud.gov

U.S. Department of the Interior

Website:	http://www.doi.gov/osdbu/
Address:	1951 Constitution Avenue, NW MS 320 SIB Washington, DC 20240
Phone number:	(202) 208-3493 (Local) 1-877-375-9927 (Toll-Free)
Fax number:	(202) 208-7444
E-mail:	DOI_OSDBU@iosl.doi.gov
Director:	Mr. Mark Oliver (202) 208-3493 mark_oliver@ios.doi.gov

Policy Analyst:	Mr. William McFadden
	(202) 208-3493
	bill_mcfadden@ios.doi.gov
Data Systems Manager:	Ms. Carol Franklin
	(202) 208-3493
	carol_franklin@ios.doi.gov
General Small Business Specialist:	Mr. LaRoy Williams
	(202) 208-3493
	laroy_williams@ios.doi.gov
General Small Business Specialist:	Ms. Chanelle Williams
	(202) 208-3493
	chanelle_williams@ios.doi.gov

U.S. Department of Justice

Website:	http://www.justice.gov/jmd/osdbu/
Address:	145 N Street, NE
	Room 8E-1009
	Washington, DC 20530
Phone number:	Primary: (202) 616-0521
	Toll Free: (800) 345-3712
Fax number:	(202) 616-1717
Director:	Mr. Robert Connolly
	(202) 616-0521
	robert.l.connolly@usdoj.gov

U.S. Department of Labor

Website:	http://www.dol.gov/oasam/programs/osdbu/regs/procurement.htm
Address:	200 Constitution Avenue, NW
	Room N-6432
	Washington, DC 20210
	osdbu@dol.gov
Phone number:	(202) 693-7297
Fax number:	(202) 693-7297
Assistant Secretary for Administration and Management Director, Small and Disadvantaged Business Utilization:	Mr. T. Michael Kerr
	(202) 693-4040
	kerr.michael@dol.gov
Director, Office of Small	Ms. Sonya Carrion

and Disadvantaged   (202) 693-7262
Business Utilization: carrion.sonya@dol.gov
Deputy Director, Office   Mr. Peter Van Steyn
of Small and   (202) 693-7292
Disadvantaged Business   vansteyn.peter@dol.gov
Utilization:
Small Business Advisor,   Ms. Jacqueline McWain
Office of Small and   (202) 693-7293
Disadvantaged Business   mcwain.jacqueline@dol.gov
Utilization:
Program Analyst, Office   Ms. Isela Martin
of Small and   (202)-693-7294
Disadvantaged Business   martin.isela@dol.gov
Utilization:
Program Analyst, Office   Mr. William Bryant
of Small and   bryant.william@dol.gov
Disadvantaged Business
Utilization:
Program Analyst, Office   Ms. Emma Jean Weaver
of Small and   (202) 693-7296
Disadvantaged Business   weaver.emma.jean@dol.gov
Utilization:

U.S. Department of State

Website: http://www.state.gov/m/a/sdbu/
Address: SA-6
                               Room L500
                               Washington, DC 20522
Phone number: (703) 875-6822
Fax number: (703) 875-6825
Director: Mr. Shapleigh Drisko
Women Business Advocate: Ms. Keisha McCormick
HUBZone Advocate: Ms. Judith Thomas
Veteran Business Advocate: Mr. Willie Taylor

U.S. Department of Transportation

Website: http://www.osdbu.dot.gov/
Address: 1200 New Jersey Avenue, SE
                               Washington, DC 20590

Phone number:	(202) 366-1930
Fax number:	(202) 366-7228
Director:	Mr. Brandon T. Neal
WOSB Rep:	Ms. Devera Redmond
	devera.redmond@dot.gov
VO/SDVOSB Rep:	Mr. Randall Nossaman
	randall.nossaman@dot.gov

U.S. Department of the Treasury

Website:	http://www.treasury.gov/osdbu/
Address:	655 15th Street
	Rm. 6W529
	Washington, DC 20220
Phone number:	(202) 622-0530
Fax number:	(202) 927-4963
Director of OSDBU:	Mr. Dan Tangherlini
	(202) 622-0530
Director Small Business Programs:	Dr. Lorraine Cole
	(202) 927-8181
Women Business Rep:	Ms. Renee Fitzgerald
	(202) 622-0530

U.S. Department of Veterans Affairs

Website:	http://www.va.gov/OSDBU/
Address:	810 Vermont Avenue, NW
	Washington, DC 20420
Phone number:	(202) 461-4300
Fax number:	(202) 461-4301
Executive Director, OSDBU:	Mr. Tom J. Leney
	(202) 461-4300
Acting Deputy Director, OSDBU:	Vacant
Deputy Director, CVE:	Ms. Gail Wegner
	Gail.Wegner@va.gov
	(202) 303-3296

VA Small Business Specialists

Bundling & eSRS Agency Coordinator:	Mr. Mark Taylor
	mark.taylor@va.gov
	(202) 461-4258
Bundling:	Mr. John Fedkenheurer

	John.fedkenheurer@va.gov
	(202) 461-4392
Bundling:	Mr. Fernando Guerra
	fernando.guerra@va.gov
	(202) 461-4251
Bundling:	Ms. Frances Bond
	frances.bond@va.gov
	(202) 461-4260
Outreach:	Ms. Linda Sitney
	linda.sitney@va.gov
	(202) 461-4262
	Mr. Lorenzo Hobbs
	lorenzo.hobbs@va.gov
	(202) 461-4255
Subcontracting & eSRS	Ms. Lynette Simmons
Alternate:	lynette.simmons@va.gov
	(202) 461-4256

U.S. Environmental Protection Agency

Website:	http://www.epa.gov/osdbu/
Address:	1200 Pennsylvania Avenue, NW
	Mail Code 1230T
	Washington, DC 20460
Phone number:	(202) 566-2075
Fax number:	(202) 566-0266
Director:	Ms. Jeanette L. Brown
Deputy Director:	Ms. Kimberly Patrick
Asbestos Small Business Ombudsman Team Lead:	Ms. Joan Rogers
Procurement Team Lead:	Mr. Lamont O. Norwood
	(202) 566-2933
Minority Academic Institutes Team Lead:	Ms. Patricia Durrant

U.S. Office of Personnel Management (OPM)

Website:	http://www.opm.gov/doingbusiness/index.aspx
Address:	1900 E Street N.W.
	Room 1330D

	Washington, DC 20415
Phone number:	(202) 606-8223
Fax number:	(202) 606-1464
Director:	Mr. Desmond Brown
	Desmond.Brown@opm.gov
	(202) 606-2862

U.S. Postal Service
Website:	http://about.usps.com/doing-business/welcome.htm
Address:	475 L'Enfant Plaza SW
	Room 1140
	Washington, DC 20260-6201
Phone number:	(202) 268-4633
Fax number:	(202) 268-7288
Manager Supplier Diversity:	Ms. Janice B. Williams-Hopkins
	(202) 268-4633
	Janice.b.williams-hopkins@usps.gov
Alternate:	Mr. Rupert R. Warner, Jr.
	(202) 268-6731
	rupert.r.warner.jr@usps.gov
Alternate:	Mr. Joseph A. Mathes
	(202) 268-2107
	joseph.a.mathes@usps.gov

U.S. Securities and Exchange Commission
Website:	http://www.sec.gov
Address:	100 F Street, NE
	Mail Stop 2900
	Washington, DC 20549
Phone number:	1 (855)732-6694
Email:	VendorOutreach@sec.gov
Supplier Diversity:	Ms. Tiffany Levy
	Supplier Diversity Officer
	Office of Minority and Women Inclusion
Small Business:	Ms. Angela Trimmier
	Small Business Rep
	(202) 551-8719

Source: http://www.osdbu.gov/members.html

6   111 - 120   Navigating GSA / Procurement Vehicles

Navigating
GSA / Procurement Vehicles

❧

Acquisition Central provides the users with the ability to select his/her desired Agency Recurring Procurement Forecast. It is divided up into four drop-down boxes. They are titled: Home Page, Small Business Information, Business Opportunities, and Procurement Forecast.

http://www.acqnet.gov/comp/procurement_forecasts/index.html

When navigating GSA's home page there are numerous tabs one can click to go to various links. Some of the tabs include: information about GSA such as the staff directory and jobs, upcoming events, travel resources, GSA regulations, and GSA references and reports, just to name a few. Some of the more important tabs that are essential when doing business with the
government are: E-Library, GSA Advantage, First Gov, and Ebuy.

E-Library
To access e-Library, click on the link titled "Schedules e-Library", located under the heading "GSA contracts and schedules" on the left hand side of the GSA home page. Schedules e-Library is the online source for the latest contract award information for GSA and Department of Veterans Affairs (VA) Schedules, as well as Government Wide Acquisition Contracts (GWACs). Access to Schedules e-Library is available 24 hours a day, 7 days a week. Schedules e-Library provides information on which suppliers have a contract and what items are available, by offering various search options—i.e., Contractor/Manufacturer Name, Contract Number, Special Item Number (SIN), Schedule Number, GWAC Name, or Keywords. Schedules e-Library also provides an Alphabetical Listing of Available Contractors, allowing customers to easily locate all

Schedule contracts and GWACs for a particular company. An updated Category Guide is designed to facilitate searches for specific groups of items.

Other features include:

- Access to information on millions of supplies and services

- Information on the latest Schedule program changes, including an "In the Spotlight" news area

- Links to the Federal Supply Schedule Listing, which contains a complete list of all GSA and VA Schedules, and the Basic Schedule Ordering Guidelines

- Links to the GSA Advantage!® Online Shopping for E-Business and e-Buy, GSA's electronic Request For Quotation (RFQ) system

- Ability to download contract award information in an Excel format by Schedule, SIN, or GWAC category (functional area)

- Links to contractor web sites, e-mail addresses, and text files containing contract terms and conditions

- New and improved look for easier browsing and navigation

Clicking the Web site picture of GSA Schedules E-library brings one to the home page for Schedules E-library. Schedules e-Library is your source for the latest GSA and VA schedules and GWAC contract award information. Schedules e-Library is updated daily to provide one with the latest award information. Here one can find out who his or her's competition is for government contracts by entering information into the search engine.

GSA Advantage

To access GSA Advantage click on the link titled, "Buy Online Now with GSA Advantage", located under the heading for Government employees and agencies in the middle of the GSA home page. With millions of products and services available, GSA Advantage provides the most convenient one-stop shopping source to meet all your procurement needs.

With GSA Advantage you have:
- The most reliable resource for Federal purchasers
- The most comprehensive selection of approved products & services
- The ability to complete purchases quickly, with confidence, and at best value

One can either browse by category or search what you are looking for by typing the information required into the search engine.

First Gov
To access First Gov click on the link at the bottom of the GSA home page. First Gov is the U.S. Government's official Web portal.

With First Gov you have:
- Access to government information by topic
- A list of government organizations (federal, state, or local)
- Information on how to contact your government
- Frequently asked questions
- A reference center containing:
- Data & Statistics
- Forms
- Graphics and photos
- Laws and regulations
- Libraries

E-buy
To access E-buy, go to the following link: https://www.ebuy.gsa.gov/. GSA's latest e-Business innovation, e-Buy, is an electronic Request for Quote (RFQ) / Request for Proposal (RFP) system designed to allow Federal buyers to request information, find sources, and

prepare RFQs/RFPs online for millions of services and products offered through GSA's Multiple Award Schedule (MAS) and Government wide Acquisition Contracts (GWAC). Federal buyers can use e-Buy to obtain quotes or proposals for services, large quantity purchases, big-ticket items, and purchases with complex requirements.

Federal Acquisition Regulations (FAR)

At www.gsa.gov/far, you will be introduced to the Federal Acquisition Regulations. The Department of Defense (DoD), GSA, and the National Aeronautics and Space Administration (NASA) jointly issue the Federal Acquisition Regulation (FAR) for use by executive agencies in acquiring goods and services.

In fact, FAR is the primary regulation for use by all Federal Executive agencies in their acquisition of supplies and services with appropriated funds. It became effective on April 1, 1984, and is issued within applicable laws under the joint authorities of the Administrator of General Services, the Secretary of Defense, and the Administrator for the National Aeronautics and Space Administration, under the broad policy guidelines of the Administrator, Office of Federal Procurement Policy, Office of Management and Budget.

The following is a sample from the FAR Small Business Programs section (FAR 19), each of these sections can be explored at length at: http:// www.arnet.gov/far/current/html/FARTOCP19.html

FAR -- Part 19 Small Business Programs
- 19.000 Scope of part.
- 19.001 Definitions.

Subpart 19.1—Size Standards
- 19.101 Explanation of terms.
- 19.102 Size standards.

Subpart 19.2—Policies
- 19.201 General policy.
- 19.202 Specific policies.
- 19.202-1 Encouraging small business participation in acquisitions.
- 19.202-2 Locating small business sources.
- 19.202-3 Equal low bids.
- 19.202-4 Solicitation.
- 19.202-5 Data collection and reporting requirements.
- 19.202-6 Determination of fair market price.
-
- Subpart 19.3—Determination of Small Business Status for Small Business Programs
- 19.301 Representations and rerepresentations.
- 19.301-1 Representation by the offeror.
- 19.301-2 Rerepresentation by a contractor that represented itself as a small business concern.
- 19.301-3 Rerepresentation by a contractor that represented itself as other than a small business concern.
- 19.302 Protesting a small business representation or rerepresentation.
- 19.303 Determining North American Industry Classification System (NAICS) codes and size standards.
- 19.304 Disadvantaged business status.
- 19.305 Protesting a representation of disadvantaged business status.
- 19.306 Protesting a firm's status as a HUBZone small business concern.
- 19.307 Protesting a firm's status as a service-disabled veteran-owned small business concern.
- 19.308 Solicitation provisions and contract clauses.
-
- Subpart 19.4—Cooperation with the Small Business Administration
- 19.401 General.

- 19.808-2 Competitive.
- 19.809 Preaward considerations.
- 19.810 SBA appeals.
- 19.811 Preparing the contracts.
- 19.811-1 Sole source.
- 19.811-2 Competitive.
- 19.811-3 Contract clauses.
- 19.812 Contract administration.

Subpart 19.9—[Reserved]

Subpart 19.10—Small Business Competitiveness Demonstration Program
- 19.1001 General.
- 19.1002 Definitions.
- 19.1003 Purpose.
- 19.1004 Participating agencies.
- 19.1005 Applicability.
- 19.1006 Exclusions.
- 19.1007 Procedures.
- 19.1008 Solicitation provisions.

Subpart 19.11—Price Evaluation Adjustment for Small Disadvantaged Business Concerns
- 19.1101 General.
- 19.1102 Applicability.
- 19.1103 Procedures.
- 19.1104 Contract clause.

Subpart 19.12—Small Disadvantaged Business Participation Program
- 19.1201 General.
- 19.1202 Evaluation factor or subfactor.
- 19.1202-1 General.
- 19.1202-2 Applicability.

- 19.1202-3 Considerations in developing an evaluation factor or subfactor.
- 19.1202-4 Procedures.
- 19.1203 Incentive subcontracting with small disadvantaged business concerns.
- 19.1204 Solicitation provisions and contract clauses.

Subpart 19.13—Historically Underutilized Business Zone (HUBZone) Program
- 19.1301 General.
- 19.1302 Applicability.
- 19.1303 Status as a qualified HUBZone small business concern.
- 19.1304 Exclusions.
- 19.1305 HUBZone set-aside procedures.
- 19.1306 HUBZone sole source awards.
- 19.1307 Price evaluation preference for HUBZone small business concerns.
- 19.1308 Contract clauses.

Subpart 19.14—Service-Disabled Veteran-Owned Small Business Procurement Program
- 19.1401 General.
- 19.1402 Applicability.
- 19.1403 Status as a service-disabled veteran-owned small business concern.
- 19.1404 Exclusions.
- 19.1405 Service-disabled veteran-owned small business set-aside procedures.
- 19.1406 Sole source awards to service-disabled veteran-owned small business concerns.
- 19.1407 Contract clauses.

7   121 - 134   Target Markets & Relationship Building

Target Market
& Relationship Building

❧

Target Markets

There are three customers you should target with your marketing efforts:

1. **Procurers** (including contracting officers/specialists)
2. **Influencers** (including program managers/high-level decision makers)
3. **End Users**

These customers are direct recipients of your services and each customer, regardless of their specialty or area of interest, expects the same basic features and services when procuring services.

1. Procurers are identified as contracting officers, contracting specialists, acquisition/policy shop personnel or others who actually select the procurement methods and conduct the procurement. The procurers have substantial authority to determine the procurement method, but they also must consider the needs of the influencers and organizational policies. However, they are also guided by self-interest to be seen as an indisposable person (not position). While awareness is an issue among procurers, the primary impediment to successfully marketing to this group is their lack of knowledge about how and when to use the schedules process.

   The contracting officer/specialists are the "gate-keepers" to the program managers and end users. The program managers know what they want, but turn to their contracting specialist to get the materials/services they need and advise on the best way to procure those services. This makes the contracting officer/ specialist a key customer because of their influence over the project manager/end user and their responsibility for selecting the contracting method.

GSA has crafted one overall message to share. To ensure the success of the schedules program, it is important to continually reinforce and communicate this message with the contracting officer/specialist:

"The contracting officer/specialist is a key part of the schedules process. He/she is needed to ensure proper implementation and formulation of the task order. Even though buying services from a schedule is a very streamlined process, agencies still need qualified contracting personnel to draft the task order requests, establish blanket purchase agreements, evaluate contract proposals and make a best value decision. Schedules do not eliminate jobs; schedules are a tool to make the acquisition process easier and timelier."

2. Influencers are identified as program managers and high-level decision-makers. Program managers and end-users are individuals who have generated the requirement or are responsible for facilitating its execution. These are individuals who may exercise influence over an individual procurement or organization-wide procurement policy, but do not actually conduct the procurement process itself.

    Program managers and end-users have a stake in how the process is conducted. The method of procurement may impact the contractors who will be considered, the speed with which the procurement will be conducted, and the ease with which the contract itself will be administered. Although they may not be in a position to dictate the procurement vehicle to be used, they can likely have influence over the decision.

    High-level decision makers within a government organization view the procurement process from a broader standpoint. They may be concerned with manpower, allocation of resources, and other big-picture issues. These decision-makers may set policies that guide how procurements will be handled. Both influencers and users look to these policies to help guide them in determining the appropriateness of various procurement methodologies.

The following key message should be emphasized when communicating with program managers:

"Government agencies are being required to do more work with less staff. With GSA's schedules you can get the work done that is critical to your mission and focus on the core functions of your job. GSA's schedules cut the red tape so that you will spend more time on achieving your goals and less time on contract support and administration."

The End User is very influential in getting the most qualified contractor (in his/her opinion) on schedule. He/she has been given tight deadlines and wants the quickest way to procure these services. Most end users are confused about the procurement process and turn to their contracting specialist for help.

Whether targeting a contracting officer/specialist, a program manager or an end user, there are some messages that should be stressed to all of them. Make sure to convey the following benefits and advantages:

Ordering

- Ease of ordering
- Federal agencies can choose from a wide selection of contractors ranging from small to large, to 8(a) to woman-owned small.
- According to the Johnson & Johnson Associates, Inc. study entitled "Impact of FAR 8.4 Comparative Analysis of Customer Elapsed-time Savings," ordering from schedules reduces procurement lead-time and administrative costs. Schedule

orders average 15 days while an open-market procurement averages 268 days.

- Meets all applicable regulations and competition requirements (including FAR & Competition In Contracting Act).
- FedBizOpps (FBO) synopsis is not required.
- Order limitations have been removed.
- The government issued purchase card, GSA SmartPay, can be used to make purchases.

Pricing

- Schedule pricing is guaranteed to be fair and reasonable.
- Flexible pricing.
- Discount volume pricing. Target Markets & Relationship Building

Control of solutions

- Access to industry leaders.
- Contractor teaming arrangements allow agencies to customize solutions.
- Ordering agency maintains a direct relationship with the contract service provider. FSS is not involved in the process except to initially establish the schedule contracts.
- Orders placed under the schedule program can count towards the Agencies' socioeconomic goals and accomplishments.
- Protests are less likely.
- Communicate with GSA about which contractors you would like to see on schedule and we will reach out to those companies.

Relationship Building
with the Government

❧

General Guidelines

Do

1. Safeguard proprietary, Privacy Act, and other sensitive and nonpublic information. Release of certain types of information to unauthorized contractor employees to analyze, create charts and graphs, enter into databases, etc., could violate the Procurement Integrity law, the Trade Secrets Act, the Privacy Act, or other law/ regulation that could subject the releaser to civil and/or criminal penalties to include mandatory removal.

2. Identify possible conflicts by contractor employees to include violations of the law (including but not limited to procurement integrity statutes and regulations). Resolve inappropriate appearances created by close relationships between federal and contractor employees.

3. Identify contractor employees as such with distinctive badges ensuring that government employees and members of the public understand their status.
   a. If possible, arrange office space in such a way as to clearly identify the contractor's work area. This will help preclude any appearance of a personal service relationship between government and contractor employees.
   b. Contractor identification should also extend to e-mail accounts. E-mail should be structured to indicate that an individual is a contractor employee.

4. Be aware of intellectual property rights consequences of contractor employee work products created in the Federal

workplace. Generally, the contractor will be able to commercially exploit software or inventions that it creates in the federal workplace.

5. Maintain contact with on-site contractor employees in order to assess performance and ascertain progress or delivery status.

6. Address ethical issues promptly and confer with legal counsel.

General Guidelines

Do Not:

1. Meet with contractor to discuss requirement development. This can give the contractor an unfair advantage during the source selection.

2. Give an incumbent contractor an unfair competitive advantage by including its employees in meetings to discuss aspects of the re-competition, or by accidentally allowing the contractor's employees to overhear or gain access to planning information.

3. Require "out of scope" work, personal services, or "inherently governmental functions." The services the contractor is required to provide through its employees are set forth in the contract.

4. Use government and contractor personnel interchangeably.

5. Intervene in the contractor's chain of command.

6. Become so involved as a government official in the operations and policies of the contractor that your judgment alone forms the basis for contractor actions such as to:
    a) Selecting or recruiting contractor employees
    b) Directing, scheduling, or critiquing individual contractor tasks on a continuous basis. Supervising contractor employees
    c) Rating individual contractor employee performance

    d) Hiring or firing individual contractor employees

    e) Determining who should perform contract tasks or how they should be done

    f) Pressure contractor to use "favorite" employees, or vv insist on particular personnel actions.

7. Accept gifts from contractors unless you know the rules. Even if they work in the Federal workplace, they are "outside sources" and the rules for their gifts are very different than the rules for gifts between employees. One major difference is that contractors and their employees may not be solicited to provide or contribute to gifts where we might be able to do so from Federal employees for a retirement gift for another Federal employee.

Industrial Security

1. Proprietary information is releasable to a contractor only if protected by appropriate contract clauses and non-disclosure releases.

2. Ensure that disclosure and discussion of sensitive information is only with those who have a need to know.

3. Do not include contractor employees in discussions or otherwise give them access to information if it will violate a law or regulation (see restrictions above) concerning its release outside the Government, or if it will give their employer an improper competitive advantage.

4. When you are in a meeting in which advanced acquisition or sensitive information is to be discussed, ensure you know who the participants are. If in doubt, ask!

5. Be aware of the environment around you. Do not discuss sensitive information in areas that are not secure (i.e. bathrooms, hallways, cafeterias, etc). Do not leave sensitive

information in an area where contractor employees may observe the information (i.e. your desk or work area).

6. Consult cognizant legal counsel if there is any question regarding release of sensitive information.

7. Contractor employees should not be placed in a position of liability for property over which they have no contractual authority, accountability or control.

8. Contractor employees cannot be delegated responsibilities for end-of-day security checks unless their contract specifically provides for it. Many times competing contractors occupy the same work area when contractually requiring one contractor to perform end-of-day security checks over another contractor; under these circumstances, a contracting officer must exercise extreme caution when adding a contract end-of-day security check requirement.

9. Legal problems could result if a contract employee obtained access to classified, sensitive unclassified, or company proprietary information. Identification of Contractor Employees Identify contractors on correspondence, in telephone conversations, and in meetings they attend.

Recognition and Awards

1. Do not become involved with the contractor's management of its employees. Contractors supervise their employees and we must allow them to decide the best method and forum for rewarding them. Do not bypass the contractors' management to present "letters of appreciation" directly to the contract employee. Coordinate the "letter of appreciation" with the contracting officer and let the contractor make the presentation to the contract employee.

2. Interact consistently with the contractor through the contracting officer. Although a contractor may be doing outstanding work in one area, the contracting officer may be taking corrective action to resolve deficiencies in other areas of the same contract. The conflicting signals may confuse the contractor and any outside parties who attempt to resolve the situation.

3. Ensure contract performance is within the scope of the contract. Recognizing a contractor for something above and beyond the tasks we are paying for could result in a claim for additional funds.

Identification of Contractor Employees

1. Contract employees may not be tasked, or asked to volunteer or organize morale building events.
2. Government officials are not authorized to grant "administrative leave" or expend government resources to compensate contractor employees to attend Government-sanctioned morale building activities (i.e. picnics, golf outings, holiday parties, sports day events, fitness time).

Gifts

1. Federal employees cannot accept items that qualify as gifts from contractor employees. "Gifts" are defined in the Joint Ethics Regulation. Consult with legal.
2. Federal employees cannot solicit gifts from contractor employees (i.e. retirement or any other gifts for government employees).

Use of Government Resources

1. Contract employees may use government resources for official business when authorized to do so by the contracting officer or his/her representative.
2. Contract employees may not use government resources in violation of any statute, regulation, rule, or policy.

Training

1. The government may provide training to contract employees if required by the contract and it doesn't create an appearance that the government is favoring one contractor over another.
2. Generally a "gift" of training offered by a contractor is prohibited. Government employees should contact their ethics counselor before accepting a "gift" of training.
3. Training provided by a contractor in accordance with a statement of work is not considered a "gift."

Transportation and Travel

1. For fixed price contracts, contractor and government employees should not share transportation.
2. For cost reimbursement contracts, it is permissible in certain circumstances for contractor and government employees to share transportation.
3. Official travel by government employees must be funded by the Federal Government directly or through a contract, unless the travel or transportation services are accepted or processed in accordance with gift acceptance procedures.
4. Personal travel or transportation service provided by a contractor is considered a gift to the government employee from a prohibited source. It may only be accepted if one of the exceptions allowing the acceptance of a gift from prohibited sources applies or if the government employee pays fair market value.

5. Contractor transportation provided for official business may be accepted in advance by an appropriate agency official as a gift to the government.

Steps to Relationship Building with the Federal Government
1. Feasibility Study

It is entirely possible there are corporate entities and government agencies who could become direct customers for you. What seems even likelier is that there are suppliers to these groups that you should be seeking out as well. Do your homework and be direct. Identify up to 10 diverse companies and three to four government agencies procuring minority contracts that you'd like to do business with. Read up on them; find out who the purchasing agents are and investigate where they post their RFPs (requests for proposals). Before responding, read the RFPs and learn what will be required of you. For instance, you may have to obtain your MBE certification, increase the amount of your insurance, and provide references.

Write them a short e-mail or letter, or call and simply have them answer the question as to whether or not they have RFPs to respond to or what their requirements are to do business with you. As you know, many have their supplier development Target Markets & Relationship Building program descriptions right on their Web sites. Learn what will be expected from you in terms of meeting their demand for product, delivery, and service. From this, you will have some clarity on whether or not your hunch is right and if your infrastructure can accommodate the demand from expansion. You may be surprised at some of the hidden opportunities you uncover.

2. Strategic Plan

I'm assuming you began your business with a sound business plan that has served you over the years. A good business plan, however-- one that will serve you throughout your growth-- needs to be updated. Before you begin your external campaign, it's important to get your own house in order. After you've done your feasibility work, you'll need to come up with a strategic plan for managing production--the biggest mistake I see many small businesses in your position make is taking on the work and then finding the human capital to produce and service.

Answer this: Do you have the capital to add the personnel before you get the deal, or will it be contingent upon the sale? The latter is never the best approach. Once you've put together a strategy on the inside to take on the new market (sales, marketing, production, fulfillment and so on), then it's time to put yourself out there.

3. Communication Tactic

The final step in the process, whether you're going solo or launching a strategic alliance, is to map out, very precisely and deliberately, a tactical plan for communication. How will you get the word out, and what is the word?

I like to bite off small pieces rather than swallow the whole pie. You may want to consider focusing on one industry at a time, and within that industry, a handful of particular organizations or companies. In that plan, you'll want to make as many impressions as you can. You want to be seen on the Internet and in their industry publications. You'll also want to develop some strategic marketing letters, join their association for access to members and opportunities for exposure, and establish yourself or a company spokesperson as an expert on your topic. For example, if you target the transportation industry, you may launch a campaign that talks about how the fabric (texture, color) of a seat or window cover enhances or diminishes the mood of passengers. You get the idea: Make it known how you can add value to their service or purpose.

If you're ready to get started, I recommend you evaluate the following resources:

- This link shows you how to write an effective proposal to the government, listing exactly what needs to be put into the proposal.

<http://www.gsa.gov/Portal/gsa/ep/contentview.do?contentType=GSA
_BASIC&contentId=18995&noc=T>

- This link brings you to the Department of Defense, Procurement Technical Assistance Centers that will provide assistance to business firms in marketing their products and services to the government in order to acquire contracts.

<http://www.dla.mil/db/procurem.htm>

- This link is a good source to use when you want to know where to start when you want to do business with the government. This link provides many different topics to help you get going in the right direction.

<http://www.business.gov/>

- This link shows facts about small businesses, women-owned businesses, and minority-owned businesses when dealing with government contracts and how they are important to the economy.

<http://wwwc.house.gov/smbiz/smallBusinessFacts/smallBusiness-
Facts.asp>

- This link is a resource guide that provides information on national organizations and programs that can assist small and minority-owned businesses.

< http://www.occ.treas.gov/cdd/SBRG09032003.htm

8

135 - 188

Teaming/Subcontracting
i.e. NDAs,CTAs,BPAs

Teaming/Subcontracting i.e. NDAs, CTAs, BPAs

❧

"Samples only, seek legal counsel for preparation of your forms."

A letter of Intent Sample:

To Whom It May Concern:

This is to confirm THE COMPANY's intent to subcontract its services to THE CONTRACT for the GOVERNMENT AGENCY.

In addition, should THE PRIME CONTRACTOR be successful in securing the prime contract for which this subcontract has been created, THE PRIME CONTRACTOR agrees that LIST COMPONENTS will be carried out and that those components will be completed only by THE SUBCONTRACTOR and not by any in-house or third-party providers.

THE SUBCONTRACTOR is certified with the State of _____ Bureau of Contract Administration and Business Development as a Woman-Owned Enterprise.

SUBCONTRACTOR   PRIME CONTRACTOR

_____   _____

Title   Authorized Signatory

_____   _____

Non-Disclosure Agreement

This is an Agreement, effective _____ between **Your Company** and **PERSON**. It is recognized that it may be necessary or desirable to exchange information between **Your Company** and **PERSON** for the purpose of teaming in pursuit of the solicitation of, **XXXXX**. If in the pursuit of such solicitation **PERSON** becomes an employee of **Your Company** all tenants of this NDA apply. It may be necessary for either Party to provide proprietary information to the other. It is understood that **PERSON** will not be submitting and/or discussing information regarding this proposal with any entity other than **Your Company**. Should, **Your Company** not submit a proposal, or decide not to submit a proposal; **PERSON** will no longer be bound by the exclusivity terms of this Agreement."

With respect to such information, the Parties agree as follows:

(1) "Proprietary Information" shall include, but not be limited to, performance, sales, financial, contractual and special marketing information, ideas, technical data and concepts originated by the disclosing Party, not previously published or otherwise disclosed to the general public, not previously available without restriction to the receiving Party or others, nor normally furnished to others without compensation, and which the disclosing Party desires to protect against unrestricted disclosure or competitive use, and which is furnished pursuant to this NonDisclosure Agreement and appropriately identified as being proprietary when furnished.

(2) In order for proprietary information to be disclosed by one Party to the other and protected in accordance with this NonDisclosure Agreement, it must be: (a) in writing; (b) clearly identified as proprietary information at the time of its disclosure by each page thereof being marked with an appropriate legend indicating that the information is deemed proprietary by the disclosing Party; and (c) delivered by letter of transmittal to the individual designated in Paragraph 3 below, or his designee. Where the proprietary information has not been or cannot be reduced to written form at the time of disclosure and such disclosure is made orally and with prior assertion of proprietary rights therein, such orally disclosed proprietary information shall only be protected in accordance with this NonDisclosure Agreement provided that complete written summaries of all proprietary aspects of any such oral disclosures shall have been delivered to the individual identified in Paragraph 3 below, within 20 calendar days of said oral disclosures. Neither Party shall identify information as proprietary which is not in good faith believed to be confidential, privileged, a Teaming/Subcontracting i.e. NDAs, CTAs, BPAs trade secret, or otherwise entitled to such markings or proprietary claims.

(3) In order for either Party's proprietary information to be protected as described herein, it must be submitted in written form as set forth in Paragraph (2) above to the individuals identified below:

Company Your Company

_____   _____

Name: Name:
Title: Title:
Address: Address:
Telephone No: Telephone No:
FAX No: FAX No:

(4) Each Party covenants and agrees that it will, notwithstanding that this NonDisclosure Agreement may have terminated or expired, keep in confidence, and prevent the disclosure to any person or persons outside its organization or to any unauthorized person or persons, any and all information which is received from the other under this NonDisclosure Agreement and has been protected in accordance with paragraphs 2 and 3 hereof; provided however, that a receiving Party shall not be liable for disclosure of any such information if the same:

(a) Was in the public domain at the time it was disclosed, or

(b) Becomes part of the public domain without breach of this Agreement, or

(c) Is disclosed with the written approval of the other Party, or

(d) Is disclosed after 3 years from receipt of the information, or

(e) Was independently developed by the receiving Party, or

(f) Is or was disclosed by the disclosing Party to a third Party without restriction, or

(g) Is disclosed pursuant to the provisions of a court order.

As between the Parties hereto, the provisions of this Paragraph 4 shall supersede the provisions of any inconsistent legend that may be affixed to said data by the disclosing Party, and the inconsistent provisions of any such legend shall be without any force or effect.

Any protected information provided by one Party to the other shall be used only in furtherance of the purposes described in this Agreement, and shall be, upon request at any time, returned to the disclosing Party. If either Party loses or makes unauthorized disclosure of the other Party's protected information, it shall notify such other Party immediately and take all steps reasonable and necessary to retrieve the lost or improperly disclosed information.

(5) The standard of care for protecting Proprietary Information imposed on the Party receiving such information, will be that degree of care the receiving Party uses to prevent disclosure, publication or dissemination of its own proprietary information.

(6) Neither Party shall be liable for the inadvertent or accidental disclosure of Proprietary Information if such disclosure occurs despite the exercise of the same degree of care as such Party normally takes to preserve its own such data or information.

(7) In providing any information hereunder, each disclosing Party makes no representations, either express or implied, as to the information's adequacy, sufficiency, or freedom from defect of any kind, including freedom from any patent infringement that may result from the use of such information, nor shall either Party incur any liability or obligation whatsoever by reason of such information, except as provided under Paragraph 4, hereof.

(8) Notwithstanding the termination or expiration of any Teaming Agreement executed in conjunction with this Agreement, the obligations of the Parties with respect to proprietary information shall continue to be governed by this NonDisclosure Agreement.

(9) This NonDisclosure Agreement contains the entire agreement relative to the protection of information to be exchanged hereunder, and supersedes all prior or contemporaneous oral or written understandings and agreements regarding this issue. This Non-Disclosure Agreement shall not be modified or amended, except in a written instrument executed by the Parties.

(10) Nothing contained in this NonDisclosure Agreement shall, by express grant, implication, estoppel or otherwise, create in either Party any right, title, interest, or license in or to the inventions, patents, technical data, computer software, or software documentation of the other Party.

(11) Nothing contained in this NonDisclosure Agreement shall grant to either Party the right to make commitments of any kind for or on behalf of any other Party without the prior written consent of that other Party.

(12) The effective date of this NonDisclosure Agreement shall be the date stipulated at the beginning of this Agreement..

(13) Violation (s) of this NonDisclosure Agreement by either party may result in legal action.

IN WITNESS WHEREOF, the Parties represent and warrant that this Agreement is executed by duly authorized representatives of each Party as set forth below on the date first stated above.

Company	Your Company
_____	_____
By:	By:
Name:	Name:
Title:	Title:
Address:	Address:
Telephone No:	Telephone No:
FAX No:	FAX No:

CTA

The following are all sample agreements and should be used as such. The information contained herein is copyrighted by Gallagher & Gallagher and cannot be used without any prior consent from Gallagher & Gallagher. Where copy says Your Company would be where your company name would go, and where copy says Contracting Company would be where the company information from the company you want to do business with
should go.

TEAMING AGREEMENT

THIS TEAMING AGREEMENT, entered into and made effective as of _____ by and between "**Contracting Company**", hereinafter referred to as "**Contracting Company**", and "**Your Company**" hereinafter referred to as "**Your Company**", states the nature and extent of the agreement between the parties hereto to develop and submit proposals to Federal Government Agencies, State Government Agencies, and other commercial businesses, hereinafter referred to as "Customers" related to programs for various and assorted types of work in enterprises where Contracting Company has experience and proficiency, hereinafter referred to as "Programs". The parties hereto will submit proposal for the Programs as requested by the Customers, hereinafter referred to as solicitations or requests for proposals. This agreement is for the explicit purpose of teaming for the Solicitation for FDIC Recruitment # (to be determined).

WITNESSETH:

WHEREAS, **Contracting Company** intends to submit proposals as the (to be determined) to the customers for Programs in response to unsolicited and solicited proposals, and **Contracting Company** desires to use the services of Your Company as a (to be determined) in the proposal submittal; and

WHEREAS, **Contracting Company** and **Your Company** have expertise and capabilities for the Programs; and

WHEREAS, **Contracting Company** intends to engage **Your Company** as a (to be determined) for these Programs and **Your Company** intends to accept a subcontract with **Contracting Company**, if the proposals for the Programs are accepted by the Customers, and prime contracts are awarded to (to be determined) as the consequence of said proposals.

WHEREAS, **Contracting Company** and **Your Company** have expertise and capabilities for the Programs; and

NOW THEREFORE, in consideration of the foregoing recitals, which are expressly incorporated into the body of this Teaming Agreement, and in consideration of the mutual promises hereinafter set forth, **Contracting Company** and **Your Company** do hereby covenant and agree as follows:

(1) Proposal Activities. As the proposed Prime Contractor for the Programs, Your Company shall be responsible for overall (as determined). Your Company shall prepare and submit proposals, with major contributions from Contracting Company, responsive to the requirements of the Solicitation/s.

(a) The scope of the work to be performed by the Teaming Partners under a Program shall be as negotiated in a subcontract issued under the Prime Contract awarded to (to be determined) as a result of a proposal.

(b) The Subcontractor shall furnish to the Prime Contractor, for incorporation into its proposal, accurate and complete information required for the proposal, including manuscripts, drawings, technical data, technical approach, management and organization plans or approach, qualifications and experience, personnel information and resumes, cost data, and other information as may be required by the Prime Contractor in order that a fully responsive proposal may be submitted in accordance with the requirements of the Solicitations.

(c) The Subcontractor shall assign the necessary qualified personnel who shall assist the Prime Contractor in the planning, preparation, and integration of a proposal.

(d) The Prime Contractor shall have full responsibility of submitting the proposals, and for the conduct of any negotiations. The Subcontractor, upon request, shall assist the Prime Contractor in any presentation or negotiations.

(e) Each party shall bear all expenses which it incurs in connection with the proposals, any negotiations, which may follow, and all other efforts under this Teaming Agreement. Neither party shall have any right to reimbursement or compensation of any kind from the other in connection with this Teaming Agreement and the activities pursued thereunder.

(f) Each party hereto agrees to use its best efforts to cause a prime contract to be awarded to the Prime Contractor as a consequence of the proposals to be prepared pursuant to this Teaming Agreement.

(2) Scope of Agreement. This Teaming Agreement shall relate only to Solicitations jointly agreed upon and acknowledged in writing by both parties and nothing herein shall be deemed to:

(a) Confer any right or impose any obligation or restriction on either party with respect to any other program effort or marketing activity at any time undertaken by either party hereto which does not pertain to specific solicitations; or

(b) Preclude either party hereto from independently soliciting or accepting any prime contract or subcontract not resulting from the specific Solicitations; or

(c) Limit the rights of either party to independently promote, market, sell, lease, license, or otherwise dispose of its standard products or services apart from specific Solicitations.

(3) Relationship of the Parties. This Teaming Agreement does not constitute, create, or give effect to a partnership, joint venture, or any other type of formal business entity. The rights and obligations of the parties hereto shall be limited to those expressly set forth herein. Neither party is the agent of the other and neither may bind the other.

(a) Unless, and until, this Teaming Agreement expires or is terminated as provided herein, both the Subcontractor and the Prime Contractor agree not to participate in any agreement or proposal effort of any kind with any other party in response to the Subject Solicitation.

(b) In all matters relating to this Teaming Agreement, the Subcontractor shall be acting as an independent contractor. Neither the Subcontractor nor its employees are employees of the Prime Contractor within the meaning or application of any federal, state, or local laws. The Subcontractor assumes all liabilities or obligations imposed by any such laws with respect to its employees. The Subcontractor shall not have any authority to assume or create any obligation, express or implied, on behalf of the Prime Contractor, or to represent itself as an agent, employee or other representative of the Prime Contractor.

(c) In all matters relating to this Teaming Agreement, the Sub-contractor shall be acting as an independent contractor. Neither the Subcontractor nor its employees are employees of the Prime Contractor within the meaning or application of any federal, state, or local laws. The Subcontractor assumes all liabilities or obligations imposed by any such laws with respect to its employees. The Subcontractor shall not have any authority to assume or create any obligation, express or implied, on behalf of the Prime Contractor, or to represent itself as an agent, employee or other representative of the Prime Contractor.

(4) Proprietary Data. Proprietary data shall be furnished by one party to the other only as necessary to fulfill this Teaming Agreement. Proprietary data shall be clearly marked by the furnishing party with an appropriate legend as the company-sensitive or proprietary data of the furnishing party. The receiving party shall protect such furnished data from disclosure to the same extent that it protects its own company-sensitive or proprietary information. Under no circumstances shall any such furnished data be released or disclosed to any other party (except Customers, as provided below) during the term of this Teaming Agreement, and for a period of two years following the termination of this Teaming Agreement. The parties hereto each designate the persons cited under paragraph 17 hereof as the only individuals for each party who shall receive all such data furnished under this Teaming Agreement. Proprietary data is furnished under this Teaming Agreement solely for the purpose of responding to the Subject Solicitation and carrying out any resulting contract. No other use of such data is authorized no shall be made. The Prime Contractor may incorporate proprietary data furnished to it by the Subcontractor into the proposal submitted under the Subject Solicitation, or may provide it to the Government as required during performance of the resulting contract, provided, however, that in each case the proprietary data shall be marked with restrictions, identifying and protecting such data, as are permitted by applicable regulations. The requirements of this paragraph shall not be enforceable under any of the following circumstances.

(a) The party furnishing proprietary data fails to properly mark the data or address it to the person designed to receive it.

(b) The receiving party independently develops the furnished data prior to its receipt.

(c) The proprietary data becomes lawfully known to the receiving party by means other than the receipt of same from the furnishing party, or is lawfully available from a source other than the furnishing party.

(d) The proprietary data becomes publicly known through no breach of this Teaming Agreement.

(5) Classified Information. U.S. Government classified data or information shall be provided by either party hereto to the other only as required under this Teaming Agreement or any resulting contract. All activities by the parties hereto carried out under this Teaming Agreement which pertain to classified data or information shall be consistent with and subject to the Security Regulations of the U.S. Department of Defense or other Government Agencies specified in the Solicitations.

(6) Inventions, Patents, and Copyrights. Except for such rights as may accrue to the U.S. Government or of employees of the Prime Contractor shall belong exclusively to the Prime Contractor. Except for such rights as may accrue to the U.S. Customers under the terms of Solicitations, inventions, patents, and copyrights resulting solely from the work of employees of the Subcontractor shall belong exclusively to the Subcontractor. Inventions, patents, or copyrights resulting from the joint endeavors of the parties hereto in the course of the work called for by this Teaming Agreement shall be subject to the further agreement of the parties. Except as provided in this paragraph or as set forth in Paragraph 4 hereof, nothing contained in this Teaming Agreement shall be deemed, by implication, estoppel, or otherwise, to grant any right or license in respect of any inventions, patents, or copyrights owned by either party hereto.

(7) Publicity. No publicity, public announcement, news release, or advertising shall be released by the Subcontractor or the Prime Contractor in connection with this Teaming Agreement or any proposal contemplated herein without the prior written approval of the other party. Neither party, however, shall be precluded from revealing the contents of this Teaming Agreement to Customers.

(8) Award of Prime Contract and Subcontract. If a Prime Contract is awarded to the Prime Contractor as a consequence of Proposals submitted in response to Solicitations as jointly agreed upon, the parties shall enter into good faith negotiations for a subcontract which shall contain such terms and conditions as are mutually agreeable to the parties. In that regard, it is agreed that all clauses required by the Prime Contract and applicable laws and regulations shall be included in any such subcontract. If prior Customer consent to or approval of the Subcontract is required, the Prime Contractor shall exert its best efforts to secure such approval.

(9) It is understood that the work to be allocated by (to be determined) to Subcontractor is dependent on the total amount of work which is ordered by the Customer under the Prime Contract. However, the level of effort ordered from the Subcontractor will be not more than 45% of the total labor costs ordered by the Customer under the Prime Contract. In addition, Subcontractor will assume responsibility for purchasing material and equipment and Other Direct Costs associated with the Prime Contract as specified in task orders issued by (to be determined) to Subcontractor. The subcontract level of effort will be definitized in subcontract task orders and/or the SOW during the base year, and during each option year of the Prime Contract.

(10) Cost of Litigation. In the event of any litigation arising out of this Teaming Agreement, it is agreed that each part hereto will pay its own costs incurred in prosecuting or defending against such litigation, including attorney's fees.

(11) Procurement Integrity. Subcontractor recognizes that Contracting Company is a "competing contractor" under the procurement integrity provisions of the Office of Federal Procurement Policy Act Amendments of 1988 (41 U.S.C. 423) as amended by section 814 of Public Law 101-189. Subcontractor hereby agrees that it will not engage in any of the activities prohibited by those provisions to the end that the Prime Contractor's right to award under the Solicitations or its rights under any resulting contract will not be adversely affected. It is agreed that this provision will survive the termination of this Teaming Agreement.

(12) Lobbying Activity. The Subcontractor agrees that it is not authorized to engage in communications or make any appearance with Federal Government personnel on behalf of the Prime Contractor that are attempts to influence a Government contract award decision. In that regard, the Subcontractor shall comply with the certification requirements of FAR 52.203-11 at the time of submission of its proposal.

(13) Applicable Law. Each party shall comply with all applicable federal, state, or local laws, regulations, or ordinances in effect or hereafter adopted. This Teaming Agreement shall be governed by and construed and interpreted in accordance with the substantive law of the State of Virginia. Teaming/Subcontracting i.e. NDAs, CTAs, BPAs

(14) Assignment. This Teaming Agreement or any interest herein shall not be transferred or assigned, in whole or in part, by either party without the prior written consent of the other. For the purpose of this Teaming Agreement, any corporate merger, acquisition, or similar change shall not be considered an assignment.

(15) Term and Termination. Except as expressly provided in paragraphs 4 and 11 hereof, this Teaming Agreement and all rights, duties, and obligations provided for herein shall terminate upon the earliest occurrence of any of the following:

(a) Written notice from the Customer that the Solicitation has been canceled.

(b) Award of a Prime Contract under the Solicitation to a party other than the Prime Contractor.

(c) The written agreement of both parties to terminate.

(d) The expiration of one year from the effective date of this Teaming Agreement.

(e) The refusal of the Customer to approve Your Company as Prime and Contracting Company as subcontractor for the Solicitation (again to be determined).

(f) The failure of the parties hereto to reach mutual agreement on a subcontract after a reasonable period (one year) of good faith negotiations.

(g) The commencement, voluntary or involuntary, of proceedings in bankruptcy for one of the parties, including filing under Chapter 11 of the U.S. Bankruptcy Code.

(16) Severability. In the event any portion of this Teaming Agreement is deemed invalid or unenforceable for any reason by a court of competent jurisdiction, the remaining portions of this Teaming Agreement shall remain in full force and effect.

(17) Changes. Any modification or amendment to this Teaming Agreement shall be in writing and signed by a duly authorized official of both parties hereto.

(18) Notices. Any notice or other writing required or permitted by this Teaming Agreement shall be deemed to have been sufficiently given either when personally delivered or mailed by certified or registered United States mail with postage prepaid to the individual representatives and addresses of the parties specified herein. The individuals designated below shall, unless and until otherwise specified in writing by the appropriate party, be the only individuals eligible to receive any and all written notices under this Teaming Agreement.

For: Contracting Company   For: Your Company

_____   _____

By: By:
Title: Title:
Address: Address:
Telephone No: Telephone No:
FAX No: FAX No:

(19) Entire Agreement. This Teaming Agreement constitutes the entire, complete, and final understanding and agreement between the parties and supersedes any previous understandings, commitments, or agreements, oral or written. Each party covenants that there is no agreement between itself and any other person, firm, or corporation which would cause this Teaming Agreement not to have full force and effect.

IN WITNESS WHEREOF, the parties hereto have, through duly authorized representatives, executed this Teaming Agreement effective as of the day and year indicated in the preamble.

For: Contracting Company For: Your Company

_____   _____

By: By:
Title: Title:
Signature: Signature:
Date: Date:

TEAMING AGREEMENT

This Agreement made and entered into on [DATE] by and between [COMPANY] and [YOUR COMPANY].

WHEREAS, the above identified parties, because of their diverse capabilities, have determined that they would benefit from a team arrangement between their respective organizations,

WHEREAS, this AGREEMENT is entered into to enable each party to enjoy the benefits of the other party's capabilities in areas of work which are not independently available within the respective companies; and

NOW, THEREFORE, in consideration of the mutual promises contained, the parties agree as follows:

1. **Best Effort.** Each party will exert its best efforts to produce a proposal or proposals for each task order which will cause the selection of [COMPANY] as a prime contractor for the PROGRAM and the acceptance of [YOUR COMPANY] as the teaming partner for the work assigned to [COMPANY]/[YOUR COMPANY] and each party will continue to exert its best efforts toward this objective throughout any and all negotiations concerning a proposed contract or subcontract which may follow the submission of the proposal or proposals. This requirement includes the furnishing of qualified personnel who will cooperate together in drafting a proposal.

2. **Identification.** It is understood that [COMPANY] will, in any proposal which the parties submit and in all discussions, identify [YOUR COMPANY] as a team member, and will state in the proposal or discussions the relationship of the parties as set forth and the areas of endeavor, tasks, and responsibility. Changes will be accomplished as mutually agreed to by both parties in writing.

3. Additional Members. [YOUR COMPANY] reserves the right, upon notification to [COMPANY], to add additional members to the PROGRAM team to assist in performing tasks outside the capabilities and scope of [COMPANY]'s tasks when additional members are added, [YOUR COMPANY] agrees to obtain adequate written protection of [COMPANY]'s proprietary information from the new team member(s) and vice versa.

4. **Proposal Material.** [YOUR COMPANY] will furnish, for incorporation into any proposal, all proposal material pertinent to the work assigned to [COMPANY], including, but not limited to manuscripts, art work, and cost and/or pricing data, as appropriate. [YOUR COMPANY] will provide [COMPANY], as part of its cost proposal, completed Government cost and pricing forms and certifications with detailed supporting schedules, including estimate rationale and bid rates with source data for both, in sufficient detail to permit [COMPANY]'s evaluation. Cost format and work breakdown structure will be as specified by [YOUR COMPANY].

5. **Personnel Availability.** [YOUR COMPANY] will assure availability of management and technical personnel to assist [COMPANY] in any discussions and negotiations with the Government directed toward obtaining the award of this contract if requested to do so by [COMPANY].

6. **Compensation.** Each party will bear all costs, risks, and liabilities incurred by it arising out of its obligations and efforts under this AGREEMENT during the Phase I of the proposal period; during Phase II some reimbursements may be negotiated. Neither party has any right to any payment or compensation of any kind from the other during the period before the award of the subcontract contemplated by this AGREEMENT.

7. **Form and Content.** [COMPANY] will have the sole right to decide the form and content of all documents submitted to the

Government. [COMPANY] will make reasonable efforts to ensure that [YOUR COMPANY] data is adequately portrayed and identified as [YOUR COMPANY]'s portion. [COMPANY] will afford [YOUR COMPANY] the opportunity to review that portion of the proposal which includes the effort to be performed by [YOUR COMPANY].

8. **Task Order**. When, during the period of this AGREEMENT, a prime contract is awarded to [COMPANY] as a result of the proposal, [COMPANY] will, to the extent permitted by Government rules, regulations, and applicable law, enter into good faith negotiations with [YOUR COMPANY] as a teaming partner. [COMPANY] will provide to [YOUR COMPANY] that portion of the work to be performed by [YOUR COMPANY] under the schedule and technical specifications, and at a price to be mutually agreed upon between the parties and subject to the stipulation that an agreement be reached within a reasonable period of time. The terms and conditions of the contract will be generally consistent with the terms and conditions in [COMPANY]'s contract. It is agreed that the terms and conditions will not conflict with Government rules, regulations and applicable law.

9. **Customer Contact**. It is agreed between the parties that [COMPANY] the prime contact with potential customers or interested government agencies concerning the PROGRAM. It becomes desirable for [YOUR COMPANY] to contact a potential customer or interested Government agency concerning the PROGRAM; the contact must be discussed by [COMPANY] to ensure coordination of efforts and understanding of commitments implementation of contact.

10. **Government Interface.** Although [COMPANY] is contemplated as the prime interface with the Government, any cogent communications invited by the Government directly with [YOUR COMPANY] concerning any matter involving this AGREEMENT will not be deemed to be a breach of this

AGREEMENT, provided [COMPANY] is notified in a timely manner by [YOUR COMPANY].

11. **Presentations.** [COMPANY] should be requested or is presented the opportunity to make presentations whether orally or by written communications to interested Government agencies concerning the PROGRAM, the content of the presentation will be made immediately known to [YOUR COMPANY] subject to any prohibitions or restrictions which may be imposed and [YOUR COMPANY] will support the presentations as directed by [COMPANY] and as it relates to [YOUR COMPANY]'s area of work.

12. **Publicity.** Any news releases, public announcement, advertisement, or publicity released by either party concerning this AGREEMENT, or any proposals, or any resulting contracts or subcontracts to be carried out, will be subject to prior approval of the other party, except that this AGREEMENT and the terms may be made known to the appropriate Government entity and ruling body.

13. **Internal Communication.** Correspondence or notification of an internal or intra-organizational nature exempt from prior approval. Any publicity give due credit to the contribution of each party.

14. **Organization Representative(s).** The parties each will designate in writing one or more individuals within their own organization as their representative(s) responsible to direct technical performance and discussions. Additionally, representative(s) designated within each organization that will be responsible for matters of a fiscal and or contractual nature. The representative(s) will be responsible to effectuate the requirements and responsibilities of the parties under this AGREEMENT.

15. **Confidentiality Clause**

(a) Confidential Information. For the purposes of this AGREEMENT "Confidential Information" means:

    i. the Licensor PRODUCTS and the Distributor PRODUCTS;

    ii. any business or technical information of Licensor or Distributor, including but not limited to any information relating to Licensor's or Distributor's product plans, designs, costs, product prices and names, finances, marketing plans, business opportunities, personnel, research, development or know-how;

    iii. any information that is designated by the disclosing party as "confidential" or "proprietary" or, if orally disclosed, reduced to writing by the disclosing party within thirty (30) days of the disclosure; and

    iv. the terms and conditions of this AGREEMENT

(b) Exclusions. Confidential Information does not include information that:

    i. is developed by the receiving party independently and without use of or concerning the disclosing party's Confidential Information;

    ii. is obtained by the receiving party from a third party without restriction on disclosure and without breach of a nondisclosure obligation;

    iii. is in or enters the public domain other than through the fault or negligence of the receiving party and without breach of this AGREEMENT;

    iv. the receiving party possesses before first receiving it from the disclosing party; or

    v. as legally required to be disclosed by law, at which point the disclosing party will notify the other party.

(c) Obligation. Except as required by law, each party shall maintain in strict confidence, and will not use or disclose, except as expressly permitted under this AGREEMENT, any Confidential Information received from the other party. Each party further agrees to use the same degree of care to maintain the confidentiality of all Confidential Information received from the other party that it uses to maintain the confidentiality of its own information of similar importance, but in no event will it use less than reasonable care.

16. Patents. If during the performance of this AGREEMENT, patentable inventions result, the following apply:

(a) Project Intellectual Property ("PROJECT INTELLECTUAL-PROPERTY") means the legal rights relating to inventions (including subject inventions as defined in 37 CFR 401), patent applications, patents, copyrights, trademarks, mask works, trade secrets, and any other legal protectable information, including computer software, first made or generated during the performance of this Project.

(b) Subject to the right of the Government under any ensuing contract, and except as otherwise provided, ownership of PROJECT INTELLECTUAL PROPERTY vests in the party whose personnel conceived the subject matter or first actually reduced the subject matter to practice, and the party may perfect legal protection in its own name and at its own expense. PROJECT INTELLECTUAL PROPERTY, which is jointly made, generated, or for which [YOUR COMPANY] and [COMPANY] have inseparable responsibility, jointly owned by [YOUR COMPANY] and [COMPANY] unless otherwise agreed to in writing. It is understood that the issue of jointly owned PROJECT INTELLECTUAL PROPERTY will remain as an item for further negotiation, including the appropriate assignment of any revenues and profits resulting from a product, process or other innovation or invention based on the cooperative effort of [YOUR COMPANY] and [COMPANY], a task is issued by [COMPANY] to [YOUR COMPANY]. Each party cooperates with the other to enable it to perfect its patent rights to this AGREEMENT.

(c) Background Intellectual Property ("BACKGROUND NTELLECTUAL PROPERTY") means property and the legal right of either [YOUR COMPANY] or [COMPANY], or both, developed before or independent of this AGREEMENT including inventions, patent applications, patents, copyrights, trademarks, mask works, trade secrets and any information embodying proprietary data as technical data and computer software. This AGREEMENT and does not imply that either party the right to use BACKGROUND INTELLECTUAL PROPERTY of the other concerning the AGREEMENT. It is understood that the issue of BACKGROUND INTELLECTUAL PROPERTY will remain as an item for further negotiation a task order is issued by [COMPANY] to [YOUR COMPANY].

17 Termination.

(a) This AGREEMENT remain in effect until the first of the following occurs:

    i. A decision by the management of [COMPANY] that it does not wish to participate in the PROGRAM, at any level, provided that the decision is communicated in writing to the other party at least thirty (30) days the due date of the proposal.

    ii. An official Government announcement that the PROGRAM has been canceled.

    iii. Upon the award of a prime contract for the subject RFP to a contractor(s) other than [COMPANY].

    iv. Completion of all work under this RFQ.

    v. The insolvency, bankruptcy or reorganization under bankruptcy laws, or assignment for the benefit of creditors of either party.

    vi. The suspension or debarment by the U.S. Government of [YOUR COMPANY] or [COMPANY].

(b) The termination of this AGREEMENT does not supersede the obligation of the parties with respect to the protection of the proprietary information, as detailed in the NON-DISCLOSURE AGREEMENT.

(c) When this AGREEMENT is terminated, parties are free to pursue their individual technical approach in association with the successful contractor or a third party for work, which is the subject of this AGREEMENT.

18 **Non-Competition.** Since a joint proposal will require the full cooperation of the parties, all parties agree that they will not actively participate in efforts that are competitive to this AGREEMENT nor compete independently for the PROGRAM during the Teaming/Subcontracting i.e. NDAs, CTAs, BPAs duration of this AGREEMENT. The term "active participation," includes, but is not limited to, the participation in proposal efforts or the interchange of technical data with competitors; provided, however, that the foregoing does not limit or restrict the rights of the parties from offering to sell or selling to others, their standard products or related services. It is also understood that no division of markets is attempted by this AGREEMENT.

19 **Contractor Team Arrangement.** This AGREEMENT is not intended by the parties to constitute or create a joint venture, pooling arrangement, partnership, or formal business organization of any kind, other than a contractor team arrangement as set forth in FAR part 9.6 and the rights and obligations of the parties are only those expressly set forth. No party authority to bind the other party except to the extent authorized. Nothing in this AGREEMENT for the sharing of profits or losses arising out of the efforts of any party.

20 **Assignment. This AGREEMENT** may not be assigned or otherwise transferred by either party in whole or in part without the express prior written consent of the other party, which consent will not unreasonably be withheld. The foregoing does

not apply either party change its corporate name or merges with another corporation.

21 **Modification and Waiver.** This AGREEMENT shall not be amended, modified nor extended, nor is any waiver of any right effective unless set forth in a document executed by duly authorized representatives of both {COMPANY] and {COMPANY]. The waiver of any breach of any term, covenant or condition a waiver of the term, covenant or condition for any subsequent breach of the same.

22 **Government Negotiation Rights.** Nothing is intended to affect the rights of the Government to negotiate directly with any party on any basis the Government may desire.

23 **Entire Agreement.** This AGREEMENT contains all of the agreements, representations, and understandings of the parties and supersedes and replaces any and all previous understandings, commitments, or agreements, oral or written, related to the award of a contract under the PROGRAM set forth.

24 **Enforceability.** If any part, term, or provision of this AGREEMENT held void, illegal, unenforceable, or in conflict with any law of a federal, state or local government having jurisdiction over this AGREEMENT, the validity of the remaining portions of provisions affected.

25 **Security Information.** To the extent the obligations of the parties involve access to security information, classified U.S. Government "Confidential" or higher, the provisions of all applicable Federal regulations apply.

26 **Governing Law.** The laws of the States of Pa., Va., The District of Columbia and the United States govern the validity and interpretation of this AGREEMENT and the legal relation of the parties.

The parties have caused this AGREEMENT to be executed by their duly authorized representatives.

For: [COMPANY]   For: [COMPANY]

By: By:
Title: Title:
Signature   Signature
Date   Date

Planning your Strategy:
Teaming/Sub-Contracting
GSA Sub-Contracting Directory

❧

GSA Subcontracting Directory

This directory is published as an aid to small business concerns seeking subcontracting opportunities with General Services Administration (GSA) prime contractors.

Pursuant to the Small Business Act, as amended by Public Law 95-507, large business prime contractors receiving federal contracts valued at over $1 million for construction, $500,000 for all other contracts, are required to establish plans and goals for subcontracting with small business firms. This directory is a listing of GSA contractors with subcontracting plans and goals. Companies are listed alphabetically by name within each of the eleven GSA regions. Each listing contains the company's name, products or services, address, and the name and telephone number of the small business contact within the company, in that order.

Small business concerns should not overlook procurement opportunities existing on a prime contract award basis with GSA. The eleven GSA Small Business Centers, offer information regarding these opportunities. See the accompanying list of Small Business Centers for the one nearest you. This directory is prepared by the Office of Small Business Utilization (OSBU) to assist small businesses. Questions about GSA subcontract requirements may be addressed to the regional office nearest you or the:

OSBU National Office
1800 F Street, NW,
Washington, DC 20405,
(202) 501-1021

SBA

Subcontracting Opportunities

Subcontracting with a Prime Contractor

Subcontracting or teaming with a prime contractor can be a profitable experience as well as a growth opportunity for your business. If, after assessing the capabilities and capacity of your business, you conclude that you are not ready to bid competitively for prime contracts, consider the opportunities available through subcontracting. The experience gained from performing as a subcontractor can assist you in responding to solicitations as a prime contractor. Subcontracting, however, should not be viewed only as an opportunity for less-experienced business, but also as a vehicle to enhance your qualifications to become more competitive to perform as a prime contractor.

Over the years, several laws have been passed regarding subcontracting to small business. All of these are now incorporated into Section 8(d) of the Small Business Act and, in most cases, FAR 19.7. These laws require prime contractors having contracts that exceed the simplified acquisition threshold (SAT) to provide maximum practicable subcontracting opportunities to small business, HUBZone small business, small disadvantaged business, women-owned small business, veteran-owned small business (VOS B), and service-disabled VOS B. The clause "Utilization of Small Business Concerns," must be included in all federal contracts exceeding the SAT. These laws, among other things, require that:

• On contracts more than $500,000 (or $1,000,000 for construction of a public facility) large prime contractors and other-than-small subcontractors submit subcontracting plans containing specific percentage goals for small business, HUBZone small business, small disadvantaged business, women-owned small business, VOS B, and service-disabled VOSB.

• Subcontracting plans must contain a description of the methods and efforts used to assure that small business enterprises have an equitable opportunity to compete for subcontracts.

• Contractors must submit subcontracting plans for review prior to the award of any contract. Failure to comply in good faith with its approved plan may subject the contractor to liquidated damages or termination for default.

The requirement to submit a subcontracting plan does not apply to:

• Small businesses,

• Contracts under the prescribed dollar amounts,

• Prime contracts not offering subcontracting possibilities, or

• Contracts to be performed entirely outside the United States.

Recommendations:

As a small business engaged in subcontracting, be sure you understand the terms and conditions of your contract with the prime contractor before agreeing to serve as a subcontractor.

Ask:

• How and when will I receive compensation from the prime contractor?

• How much can I rely on the prime contractor for special tools, engineering advice, information on manufacturing methods, etc.?

• How will quality control and inspection procedures be applied to my subcontract?

Find Subcontracting Opportunities

How the Government Buys

The government buys many of the products and services it needs from suppliers who meet certain qualifications. It applies standardized procedures by which to purchase goods and services. That is, the government does not purchase items or services in the way an individual household might. Instead, government-contracting officials use procedures that conform to the Federal Acquisition Regulation (FAR). The FAR is a standardized set of regulations used by all federal agencies in making purchases. It provides procedures for every step in the procurement process, from the time someone in the government discovers a need for a product or service to the time the purchase is complete. The FAR can be accessed electronically at www.arnet.gov/far.

As of October 1, 2001, the government transitioned from Commerce Business Daily (CBD) to Federal Business Opportunities (FedBizOpps) to "post" all procurement opportunities expected to exceed $25,000. FedBizOpps is a web-based application and is the government-wide point of entry to communicate its buying requirements to potential suppliers. This very important website can be accessed at
http://www.FedBizOpps.gov.

When the government wants to purchase a certain product or service, it can use a variety of contracting methods. Simplified acquisition procedures, sealed bidding, contracting by negotiation and consolidated purchasing vehicles are key contract methodologies used to purchase products and services.

Simplified Procedures

The Federal Acquisition Streamlining Act (FASA) of 1994 is intended to simplify government buying procedures. It removed many competition restrictions on government purchases of less than $100,000. Instead of full and open competition, agencies can now use simplified procedures for soliciting and evaluating bids up to $100,000. Government agencies, however, are still required to advertise all planned purchases over $25,000 in www.FedBizOpps.gov.

Simplified procedures require fewer administrative details, lower approval levels, and less documentation. New procurement reform legislation requires all federal purchases above $2,500 but under $100,000 to be reserved for small businesses, unless the contracting officer cannot obtain offers from two or more small businesses that are competitive on price, quality, and delivery. Government purchases of up to $2,500 in individual items or multiple items whose aggregate amount does not exceed $2,500 are now classified as "micro-purchases" and can be made without obtaining competitive quotes. However, these purchases are no longer reserved for small businesses. Agencies can make micro-purchases using a Government Purchase Card (typical credit card).

Sealed Bidding

Sealed bidding is how the government contracts competitively when its requirements are clear, accurate, and complete. An Invitation For Bid (IFB) is the method used for the sealed bid process. Typically, an IFB includes a description of the product or service to be acquired, instructions for preparing a bid, the conditions for purchase, packaging, delivery, shipping and payment, contract clauses to be included, and the deadline for submitting bids. Each sealed bid is opened in public at the purchasing office at the time designated in the invitation. All bids are read aloud and recorded. A contract is then awarded by the agency to the low bidder who is determined to be responsive to the government's needs. Government-wide IFBs are available daily for review at www.FedBizOpps.gov. This electronic government service also provides a direct link to the invitation.

Contracting officials search the SBA's Procurement and Marketing Access Network (PRO-Net) to identify qualified small business contractors. Therefore, any small business that wants to sell to the government should be registered on SBA's PRO-Net.

Contract Negotiation

In certain cases, when the value of a government contract exceeds $100,000 and when it necessitates a highly technical product or service, the government may issue a Request for Proposal (RFP). In a typical RFP, the government will request a product or service it needs, and solicit proposals from prospective contractors on how they intend to carry out that request, and at what price. Proposals in response to an RFP can be subject to negotiation after they have been submitted.

When the government is merely checking into the possibility of acquiring a product or service, it may issue a Request for Quotation (RFQ). A response to an RFQ by a prospective contractor is not considered an offer, and consequently, cannot be accepted by the government to form a binding contract. The order is an offer by the government to the supplier to buy certain supplies or services upon specified terms and conditions. A contract is established when a supplier accepts the offer.

Government-wide RFPs and RFQs are available daily for review at www.FedBizOpps.gov.This electronic government service also provides a direct link to the request. In most instances, the government uses oral solicitations for purchases less than $25,000, written solicitations for purchases over $25,000, and purchase cards to obtain micro-purchases less than $2,500.

One of the most significant changes government acquisition reform is the increased importance of "best value." Best value means that, rather than making awards to the lowest bidder as it generally did in the past, the government can now make awards for the item that best satisfies its needs at a slightly higher price. If purchasers are going to make an award based on best value, they must state their intent in the solicitation document and include a description of the evaluation criteria, award factors, and factors other than the price that will be considered in making a contract award.

Contracting officials search the SBA's Procurement and Marketing Access Network (PRO-Net) to identify qualified small business contractors. Therefore, any small business that wants to sell to the government should be registered on SBA's PRO-Net.

Consolidated Purchasing Programs

Most government agencies have common purchasing needs; carpeting, furniture, office machine maintenance, petroleum products, and perishable food supplies are just a few examples. Sometimes the government can realize economies of scale by centralizing the purchasing of certain types of products or services.

Acquisition Vehicles - Procurement reform has ushered numerous new and/or modified acquisition vehicles - multiple award contracts -- such as multi-agency contracts and government wide acquisition contracts (GWACs). These vehicles encourage long-term vendor agreements with fewer vendors.

The use of these contract vehicles, including expanded use of GSA schedules has increased significantly during the last few years. These popular vehicles allow government buyers to quickly fill requirements by issuing orders against existing contracts or schedules without starting a new procurement action from scratch. Further, agencies can competitively award several or multiple task order contracts to different firms for the same products and services. This practice allows federal buyers to issue orders to any one or combination of several firms with relative ease.

The General Services Administration, the Defense Logistics Agency, and the Department of Veterans Affairs administer the three largest interagency consolidated purchasing programs.

Federal Acquisition Regulations (FAR)

Understanding the government's procurement rules is critical to your success as a government contractor. The Federal Acquisition Regulations (FAR) system is the roadmap for doing business with the government

The FAR was established to codify uniform policies for acquisition of supplies and services by executive agencies. It is issued and maintained jointly, pursuant to the OFPP Reauthorization Act, under the statutory authorities granted to the Secretary of Defense, Administrator of General Services and the Administrator, National Aeronautics and Space Administration. Statutory authorities to issue and revise the FAR have been delegated to the Procurement Executives in DOD, GSA and NASA.

The FAR system is a comprehensive guide that is indexed by topic.

Contractor Responsibilities

Knowing what and how the government buys is essential if a business owner is to be successful in government contracting. Don't think, however, that you can relax once you receive the good news that you have won a contract. Your work is just beginning. If you cannot perform according to the terms of the contract, the government will not get the product or service it needs and you may find yourself in financial difficulty as well.

The first thing to do is to read the proposed contract carefully before signing it. This may look like an imposing task, as some contracts may contain many pages, depending on the type of contract and complexity of what the government is buying. However, many contract terms and conditions are "boiler plate." Once you read and understand the terms, you will be familiar with them when they appear in your next contract.

One important feature of the contract is the identity of the office that will administer it. In most federal agencies this is usually the same office that awarded the contract. In the Department of Defense, however, the contract is generally assigned to a special administering office. If you have any questions about the contract, contact the office of administration. Do not proceed and find out much later that you are not in compliance.

Specific Contract Administration Matters

While federal contracts are similar to commercial contracts, they are different in some very important ways. They contain or make reference to many general contract provisions unique to the government.

These provisions implement various statutory or regulatory requirements applicable solely to federal contracts Some of the important matters covered by these provisions are termination for default, termination for convenience, contract changes, payments; specifications, and inspection and testing. These matters are described in various parts of the Federal Acquisition Regulations. The SBA's Office of Government Contracting can assist you understanding these FAR provisions.

Termination for Default Government contracts provide that the government may cancel (terminate) your contract if:

• You fail to make delivery within the time specified in the contract,
• You fail to make progress so as to endanger performance of the contract, and/or
• You fail to perform any provisions of the contract.

Before terminating a contract for default, the contracting officer must, however, give you an opportunity to remedy defects in your performance or show why your contract should not be terminated.

If your contract is terminated for default, you are entitled only to payment at the contract's price for items accepted by the government. If the government still needs the items that you failed to deliver, it has the right to procure the same items elsewhere and, if they cost more, charge the excess costs to you. This can be a very serious and costly matter.

If you can show that your failure to deliver or to make progress is excusable, your contract will not be terminated for default. To be excusable, a delay must be beyond your control and not caused by your fault or negligence. If your contract is terminated for default and you can prove that the government's action was improper, the termination will be treated as one for the "convenience of the government."

The government may unilaterally terminate all or part of a contract for its convenience. This type of termination does not arise from any fault on the part of the contractor. Termination for convenience protects the government's interests by allowing it to cancel contracts for products that become obsolete or unnecessary.

As with terminations for default, the government must give you written notice of termination for convenience, but is not required to give advance notice. The notice of termination will usually direct you to:

• Stop work,
• Terminate subcontracts,
• Place no further orders,
• Communicate similar instructions to subcontractors and suppliers, and
• Prepare a termination settlement claim.

If you fail to follow these directions, you do so at your own risk and expense. You should also receive detailed instructions as to the protection and preservation of all property that is or may become government-owned.

After termination for convenience, the government will make a settlement with you to compensate you fully and fairly for the work you have done and any preparation made for the terminated portion of the contract. A reasonable allowance or profit is also included.

Contracts change as the needs of the government change. Government contracts contain a clause authorizing the contracting officer to unilaterally order changes in the specifications and other contract terms. The changes must be "within the general scope of the contract." The contractor is obliged to perform the contract as unilaterally changed by the contracting officer. A change is within the scope of the contract if it can be regarded as within the contemplation of the parties at the time the contract was entered into. The government cannot use a change order to change the general nature of the contract. The contractor is entitled to an equitable adjustment in price and delivery schedule if changes are ordered.

The obligation to make prompt payments for products delivered or services rendered is, generally speaking, the primary obligation of the government on a procurement contract. Payment is, naturally, of utmost importance to the small business. Your contract will specify the government office responsible for payment and will contain invoicing instructions. The more accurate your invoices, the more quickly you will be paid, so it is important to understand the payment process thoroughly. Prompt payment on all contracts serves the best interest of both the contractor and the government. Under certain circumstances if the government does not accomplish prompt payment, you can submit a request for interest payments.

Under fixed-price contracts, the method of payment can vary with the dollar value of the contract. For relatively small contracts with a single item of work, you will generally be paid the total contract price in one lump sum. Payment is made after the government accepts delivery. For larger contracts with many items, you can invoice and receive partial payments. For example, in a contract for 120 units with a delivery rate of 10 per month, you can invoice each month for the price of delivered (and accepted) items.

Larger fixed-price contracts and subcontracts where the first delivery is several months after award may contain a clause permitting you to receive progress payments based upon costs incurred as work progresses.

Because progress payments are based on work that is not completed, you must repay them if you fail to complete the work. To protect its interest, the government takes title to your work-inprocess for which progress payments have been made. To qualify for progress payments, you must have an accounting system that can accurately identify and segregate contract costs.

The federal government has exact specifications for most of the products and services it buys on a regular basis. In all likelihood, your contract will contain such precise specifications. In fact, the specifications -- which describe the government's requirements - - were contained in the invitation for bids or request for proposals on which you based your bid or proposal. Once an award is made to your company, you are contractually bound to deliver the product or service described in the specifications. Sometimes, the basic specifications will make reference to and incorporate other federal specifications. You are, of course, bound by the terms of these specifications as well as the basic specifications. Failure to deliver a product meeting these terms may result in termination of your contract by default.

Accordingly, as mentioned previously, never bid on a contract unless you have read and understood all of the specifications. Also, read the specifications again before you start work under the contract.

Inspection and Testing Government contracts provide that the government may inspect and test the items you deliver to Teaming/Subcontracting i.e. NDAs, CTAs, BPAs determine if they conform to contract requirements and specifications. The government will not accept a contractor's product unless it passes inspection. The type and extent of inspection and testing depend largely on what is being procured.

In addition to knowing the item you are manufacturing or the service you are providing, you should have a working knowledge of government contracting procedures, some of which are explained in this publication. You should also be aware of the following:

• The government conducts its business through authorized agents called contracting officers. Only a contracting officer has authority to bind the government, unless you are otherwise advised in writing. However, even contracting officers have limits on their authority; so do not hesitate to make sure of the authority of the person with whom you are dealing.

• Government procurement has historically been used as a vehicle for advancing various national, social, and economic objectives. As a government contractor, you will be required to comply with the labor standards statutes (Service Contract Act, Contract Work Hours and Safety Standards Act, etc.) and other statutes advancing national socio-economic objectives, except for certain contracts where such legislation is specifically stated as non-applicable.

• You should become familiar with the contract provisions protecting the integrity of the government procurement process.

These provisions include the "officials not to benefit" clause, the "anti-kickback" provisions, the "gratuities" clause, etc.

• Disputes between you and the contracting officer may occur under the contract. Federal contracts contain a clause setting forth procedures to resolve disputes. If the contracting officer issues a decision that is not satisfactory to you, you must make a timely appeal or the decision becomes final. The Board of Contracts Appeal hears appeals.

• Do not attempt to build something bigger, better or different than called for by the contract. If you do, it may be too big or too heavy or may not fit and the government will not accept it. Simply comply with the contract terms, particularly the specifications.

• If your contract requires production, establish a production control schedule to assure that you will have the right materials in-house at the right time to meet delivery requirements. Make sure to place any subcontracts promptly and schedule delivery of subcontracted items carefully to avoid over-or-under stocking. If it appears you will not meet your schedule, notify the administration office immediately to obtain assistance. Failure to deliver on time gives the government the right to cancel your contract, with possibly disastrous results to you.

• One of the first things that must be done by a small business is to market to the Federal government. The best ways to start include registering on SBA's PRO-Net database, and contracting the agency's office of small and disadvantaged business utilization (OSDBU).

• Being e-commerce savvy is very important in doing business with the federal government. For example, if you want to do business with the Department of Defense, you must be able to invoice and receive payments electronically. Therefore, small business owners interested in doing business with the federal government should master electronic commerce.

Identify Your Business

Clearly defining your business is important for accurate representation of your firm when submitting contract proposals. In addition, such identification can serve as a marketing strategy. Government agencies are required to establish and (strive to) meet a variety of small business procurement goals. For example, an agency may be looking for a woman-owned business to fulfill specific contract requirements and help it achieve a government wide, 5% goal of contracting with women-owned small businesses.

Are you a small business?

Small business size standards are based on the North American Industry Classification System (NAICS).

Are you a woman-owned business?

A woman-owned business is defined as a business that is owned and controlled 51% or more by a woman or women. Currently, a woman-owned certification process is not required for federal contracts. When submitting a proposal, simply self-certify by checking the appropriate box.

Are you a veteran-owned business?

A veteran-owned business is defined as a business that is owned 51% by a veteran(s). There is no veteran-owned certification process to complete, simply self-certify.

Are you a service-disabled veteran-owned business?

A service-disabled business is defined as a business that is owned 51% by one or more service-disabled veterans. The Veterans Administration confirms disability.

Are you a small disadvantaged business? (SDB)

A small disadvantaged business is defined as a firm that is 51% or more owned, controlled, and operated by a person(s) who is socially and economically disadvantaged. African Americans, Hispanic Americans, Asian Pacific Americans, Subcontinent Asian Americans, and Native Americans are presumed to qualify. Other individuals can qualify if they show by a " preponderance of the evidence" that they are disadvantaged.

Are you a HUBZone business?

The Small Business Administration's HUBZone Program is designed to promote economic development and employment growth in distressed areas by providing access to more federal contracting opportunities. HUBZone is defined as a "Historically Underutilized Business Zone". Certified small business firms will have the opportunity to negotiate contracts and to participate in restricted competition limited to HUBZone firms.

North American Industry Classification System (NAICS)

The SIC will be replaced by the six-digit North American Industry Classification System (NAICS) code. The new NAICS system was developed to reorganize business categories on a production/process-oriented basis. The purpose behind the creation of the NAICS classification system is specifically for governmental regulations and census reports.

Federal Supply Classification (FSC) - identifies products

The federal government uses numeric federal supply class (FSC) codes to describe the supplies, products and commodities it purchases.

Works Cited

❧

A-Z Agency Index
FirstGov.gov
The U.S. Government's Official Web Portal 28 July 2006.
<http://www.firstgov.gov/index.shtml>

AcqWeb Acquisition, Technology, and Logistics
The Office of the UnderSecretary of Defense for
Acquisition,Technology, and Logistics. 2 Aug. 2006.
<http://www.acq.osd.mil/>

Agency Recurring Procurement Forecasts
Acquisition Central. 2 Aug. 2006.
<http://www.acqnet.gov/comp/procurement_forecasts/index.html>
Bellis,

Mary. Nondisclosure Agreements.
1 Aug. 2006.
<http://inventors.about.com/od/nondisclosure/a/Nondisclosure.htm
>

Benefits and Advantages of Using Blanket
Purchase Agreements GSA. 1 Aug. 2006.
<http://www.gsa.gov/Portal/gsa/ep/content-
View.do?programId=10013&channelId=13462&ooid=8101&content
Id=21336&pageTypeId=8199&contentType=GSA_BASIC&program
Page=%2Fep%2Fprogram%2FgsaBasic.jsp&P=FX7>

Best Practice
Federal Government. 2 Aug. 2006.
<http://www.osdbu.gov/Assets/PDF/Best%20Practices.pdf>

Blanket Purchase Agreement
GSA. 1 Aug. 2006.
<http://www.gsa.gov/Portal/gsa/ep/channelViewo?pageType
Id=8199 &channelPage =%2Fep%2Fchannel%2FgsaOverview.
jsp&channelId=-13462>

Blanket Agreement Purchase Format
GSA. 1 Aug. 2006.
<http://www.gsa.gov/Portal/gsa/ep/contentView.
do?programId=10013&
channelId=13462&ooid=8101&contentId=85
94&pageTypeId=8199&contentType=GSA_BASIC&programPage=
%2F
ep%2Fprogram%2FgsaBasic.jsp&P=FX7>

CCR Handbook
Central Contractor Registration. 2 Aug. 2006.
<http://www.ccr.gov/handbook.asp#Information_Needed>

Certification(s) or Qualification(s) Requirements
SBA. 1 Aug. 2006.
<http://www.sba.gov/certifications/>

Code of Federal Regulations
U.S. Government. 2 Aug. 2006.
<http://www.sba.gov/library/cfrs/13cfr124.html>

Conferences and Seminars
GSA. 23 Aug. 2006.
<http://www.gsa.gov/Portal/gsa/ep/contentView.
do?contentType=GSA_OVERVIEW&contentId=10073&noc=T>

Contractor Responsibilities.
SBA 1 Aug. 2006.
<http://www.sba.gov/businessop/basics/contractor.html>

Contractor Team Agreements
1 Aug. 2006.
<http://www.gsa.gov/Portal/gsa/ep/channelView.
do?pageTypeId=8199 &channelPage=%2Fep%2Fchannel%2
FgsaOverview.jsp&channelId=-13527>

Davis-Bacon Wage Determinations
U.S. Government Printing Office. 10 Aug. 2006.
<http://www.gpo.gov/davisbacon/>

Deo, Mark
2 Aug 2006.
<http://www.sbanetwork.org/>

Direct Marketing Association
2 Aug 2006.
<http://www.the-dma.org/>

EBuy
GSA. 2 Aug. 2006.
<https://www.ebuy.gsa.gov/advgsa/advantage/ebuy/start_page.do>

Elements of a Contractor Team Arrangement Document
GSA. 1 Aug. 2006.
<http://www.gsa.gov/Portal/gsa/ep/contentView.do?programId=101
57&channelI d=13527&ooid=8124&contentId=18047&pageTypeId
=8199&
contentType=GSA_BASIC&programPage=%2Fep%2Fprogram
%2FgsaBasic.jsp&P=FX7>

Establishment of Blanket Purchase Agreement
GSA. 1 Aug. 2006.
<http://www.gsa.gov/Portal/gsa/ep/contentView.do?programId=100
13&channelId=13462&ooid=8101&contentId=21297&pageTypeId=
8199&contentType=GSA_BASIC&programPage=%2Fep%2Fprogra
m%2FgsaBasic.jsp&P=FX7>

Expo 2006
GSA. 2 Aug. 2006.
<http://www.expo.gsa.gov/>

FedBizOpps
Federal Business Opportunities. 2 Aug. 2006.
<http://www.fedbizopps.gov/>

Federal Procurement Data System
GSA. 2 Aug. 2006.
<https://www.fpds.gov/>

FedWorld.com
A Program of the United States Department of Commerce. 2 Aug.
2006. <http://www.fedworld.gov/>

Free Online Courses
SBA. 1 Aug. 2006.
<http://www.sba.gov/training/courses.html#GOVERNMENT%20C
ONTRACTING>

Frequently Asked Questions
GSA. 1 Aug. 2006.
<http://www.gsa.gov/Portal/gsa/ep/contentView.do?faq=yes&pageT
ypeId =8199&contentId=8124&contentType=GSA_OVERVIEW>

Frequently Asked Questions
SBA. 1 Aug. 2006.
<http://www.sba.gov/GC/FAQs-mar2005.pdf>

Frequently Asked Questions
SBA. 1 Aug. 2006.
<http://www.sba.gov/GC/FAQs-mar2005.pdf>

Garver, Michael et al.
"Seven keys to better forecasting." Business Horizons.
Sept.-Oct.1998. 44-52. 2 Aug. 2006.
<http://bus.utk.edu/ivc/forecasting/articles/Seven%20Keys%20to%2
0Better%20Forecasting%2011-02.pdf>

GEIA
Government Electronics & Information Technology Association.
2 Aug. 2006.
<http://www.geia.org/>

General Services Administration
GSA. 2 Aug. 2006.
< http://www.gsa.gov/>

Glossary
National Standards for Civics and Government. 27 July 2006.
<http://www.civiced.org/stds_glossary.html>

Glossary of Congressional and Legislative Terms
The Capital Net. 28 July 2006.
<http://www.thecapitol.net/glossary/index.html>

Glossary of Legislative Terms
Legislative Counsel Bureau. 1 Aug. 2006.
<http://www.sen.ca.gov/ftp/access/guides/ap3glos.htm>

Glossary of Local Government Terms
Student Voices. 28 July 2006.
<http://student-voices.org/glossary/>

Government Contracting
SBA. 2 Aug. 2006.
<http://www.sba.gov/GC/indexprograms-cawbo.html>

Government Glossary
Monroe County Women's Disability Network.
27 July 2006.
<http://www.mcwdn.org/GOVERNMENT/Glossary.html>

GSA Advantage
GSA. 23 Aug. 2006.
<https://www.gsaadvantage.gov/>

GSA Expo
GSA. 23 Aug. 2006.
<http://www.expo.gsa.gov/>

Gulf Coast Business Matchmaking
SBA. 10 Aug. 2006.
http://www.sba.gov/gulf/gulfstates_bmm.html>

Helping U.S. Companies Export
Export.Gov. 10 Aug. 2006.
<http://www.export.gov/>

Hollis, Deborah and Norberto Lozoya-Escobar.
List of Government Acronyms.
Government Publications Library at University of
Colorado at Boulder. 28 July 2006.
<http://ucblibraries.colorado.edu/govpubs/a-z/alpha.htm>

How the Government Buys
SBA. 1 Aug. 2006.
http://www.sba.gov/businessop/basics/buys.html

HQ PACAF/LGC Guide For Maintaining Proper Government-Contractor
Relationships. 2 Aug. 2006.
<https://www.safaq.hq.af.mil/contracting/affars/5303/training/gov-con-relations.doc>

HUBZone Program Application Guide
SBA Your Small Business Resource. 2
Aug. 2006.
<https://eweb1.sba.gov/hubzone/internet/general/application-guide.cfm>

Identify Your Business
SBA.1 Aug. 2006.
<http://www.sba.gov/businessop/basics/identify.html>

Labor Standards for Government Contracts.
U.S. Army Corps of Engineers. 10
Aug. 2006.
<http://www.nao.usace.army.mil/redesign/Executive/Executive%20Offices/office_of_counsel/Laborstds.asp>

Manufacturing and Services
U.S. Department of commerce International Trade
Administration. 10 Aug. 2006.
<http://www.trade.gov/mas/>

National Contact Center
FCIC Federal Citizen Information Center.
2 Aug. 2006.
<http://www.pueblo.gsa.gov/call/phone.htm/>

Northern New Mexico Supplier Alliance
Los Alamos National Laboratory.
2 Aug. 2006.
<http://www.nnmsa.org/>

Office of Personnel Management
The Federal Government's Human Resources Agency.
2 Aug. 2006.
<http://www.opm.gov/>

Office of Small Business Utilization Overview
GSA. 2 Aug. 2006.
<http://www.gsa.gov/Portal/gsa/ep/programView.do?programId=96
01&programPage=%252Fep%252Fprogram%252FgsaOverview.jsp&
P=&pageTypeId=8199&ooid=10382&channelId=-13325>

Ordering From Blanket Purchase Agreements
GSA. 1 Aug. 2006.
<http://www.gsa.gov/Portal/gsa/ep/contentView.do?programId=100
13&
channelId=13462&ooid=8101&contentId=21078&pageTypeId=819
9&contentType=GSA_BASIC&programPage=%2Fep%2Fprogram%
2FgsaBasic.jsp&P=FX7>

Proposal
GSA. 10 Aug. 2006.
<http://www.gsa.gov/Portal/gsa/ep/contentview.do?contentType=G
SA_BASIC&contented=18995&noc=T>

Procurement Technical Assistance Centers
Department of Defense.
10 Aug. 2006.
<http://www.dla.mil/db/procurem.htm>

Resource Guide
SBA. 10 Aug. 2006.
<http://www.sba.gov/library/successXV/17resource2.htm>

Role in the economy
House of Representatives. 10 Aug. 2006.
<http://wwwc.house.gov/smbiz/smallBusinessFacts/smallbusinessfac
ts.asp>

Schedules E-Library
GSA. 23 Aug. 2006.
<http://www.gsaelibrary.gsa.gov/>

Small Business Resource Guide
Comptroller of the Currency Administrator of National Banks.
10 Aug. 2006.
<http://www.occ.treas.gov/cdd/SBRG09032003.htm>

Subcontracting Director
GSA. 1 Aug. 2006.
<http://www.gsa.gov/Portal/gsa/ep/contentView.do?contentType=
GSA_BASIC&contentId=13765&noc=T>

Teaming Agreement
Gallagher Gallagher, Inc. 1 Aug. 2006.
<http://www.gallagher-gallagher.com

The Association For Enterprise Integration
10 Aug. 2006.
<http://www.afei.org/>

The Basics
SBA. 10 Aug. 2006.
<http://www.sba/gov/businessop/index/html>

The Coalition for Government Procurement
2 Aug. 2006.
<http://www.coalgovpro.org/>

The official business link to the U.S. Government
10 Aug. 2006.
<http://www.business.gov/>

The White House
U.S. Government. 2 Aug. 2006.
<http://www.whitehouse.gov/error-404.html>

U.S. Blue Pages

Federal Government. 2 Aug. 2006.

<http://www.usbluepages.gov/>

United States House of Representatives

U.S. Government. 2 Aug. 2006.

<http://www.house.gov/>

United States Senate

U.S. Government. 2 Aug. 2006.

<http://www.senate.gov/>

U.S. SBA

2 Aug 2006.

http://www.sba.gov/calendar/

ABOUT DAISY GALLAGHER

Ms. Daisy Gallagher is the CEO and Founder of Gallagher & Gallagher Worldwide, Inc. an award winning integrated marketing firm. She also serves the firm's Chief Global Strategy Officer. In 1990, Ms. Gallagher founded her firm and almost immediately began working in the government contracting arena. She has worked with numerous agencies on initiatives, including the United States Department of Defense (Army, Navy, Air Force) United States Veterans Administration, United States Department of Justice, United States Postal Inspection Service, United States Office of Personnel Management, the United States General Services Administration, United States Alcohol Tobacco and Firearms, United States Department Of Energy, the White House and others. She works on public outreach and public education initiatives, sustainable integrated marketing and recruitment Branding initiatives. Her firm is holds two GSA schedules, she was the first woman business, the first in the State of Pennsylvania and the first of twenty in the nation to be awarded the AIMS schedule. Ms. Gallagher has received numerous recognitions and awards in her career including named One of the Top Five Women Businesses in Nation by U.S. Small Business Administration, Named Best 50 and Top 25 Women in Business by Pennsylvania Department of Community and Economic Development. She was also named U.S. Small Business Administration Small Business Person of the Year, University of Scranton SBDC Woman Entrepreneur of the Year, Greater Pocono Chamber of Commerce Citizen of the Year, the recipient of Women In Communication SARAH Award for Public Relations, and her firm also earned the Public Relations Society Overall Excellence Awards for two consecutive years for full government campaign initiatives. Ms. Gallagher was honored as a Paul Harris Fellow and as the first woman Rotarian of the Year in her Rotary Club's 75 year history. She was honored in Greece and presented by EAWC and the Greek government with the ARTEMIS award. Ms. Gallagher has also earned numerous citations and recognitions from Congress and her community for business growth and community involvement. The firm has also received international recognition and multiple national awards in every category of its industry over its long stance in business. Ms. Gallagher is Senior Advisor and Keynote Speaker/Trainer. She is a leading expert in Sustainable Brand Marketing. Her most received educational achievements include both Advanced Masters in Project Management and Masters in Project Management certificates from Villanova University, training in NLP and as a success Coach. In addition, she is International Board Certified Clinical Practitioner (CHT) and the author of numerous published works. The Government Contractor's Resource Guide, was compiled as a result of more than two decades of her own experience as a small business in government contracting and to assist other small businesses who find at times it an overwhelming process and either stop after a short time due to lack of awards or simply do not know where to begin. In particular, like herself, there is a focus on information to help set asides, minority, woman owned, veterans, and those in labor surplus areas, who wish to help their communities and create jobs while growing or maintaining their business through these opportunities. She is also author of the popular book entitled "How to Succeed in a Testosterone World without Losing Estrogen," which focuses on providing research, lessons learned, and strategies to empower women for success in business. Ms. Gallagher has been a small business champion and community leader, she has served and chaired numerous Boards, including Industry Boards, Economic & Charitable Non Profit boards and served on local, state and federal government councils and committees; including a federal agency's Industry Government Council Steering Committee and Small Business Advisory Committee for a federal agency.

www.ingramcontent.com/pod-product-compliance
Lightning Source LLC
Chambersburg PA
CBHW061221220326
41599CB00025B/4714